The NEW Fun Encyclopedia

Volume 1. *Games*

Volume 2. *Parties and Banquets*

Volume 3. *Home and Family Fun*

Volume 4. *Skits, Plays, and Music*

Volume 5. *Sports and Outdoor Fun*

The NEW Fun Encyclopedia

Volume 4
Skits, Plays, and Music

E. O. Harbin

revised by
Bob Sessoms

ABINGDON PRESS
Nashville

THE NEW FUN ENCYCLOPEDIA
VOLUME IV. SKITS, PLAYS, AND MUSIC

Library of Congress Cataloging in Publication Data

(Revised for vol. 4)
HARBIN, E. O. (ELVIN OSCAR), 1885–1955
The new fun encyclopedia.
Rev. ed. of: The fun encyclopedia. © 1940.
Includes bibliographies and indexes.
Contents: v. 1. Games—v. 2. Parties and banquets—[etc.]—v. 4. Skits, plays, and music.
1. Amusements—Collected works. 2. Games—Collected works. 3. Entertaining—Collected works. I. Sessoms, Bob. II. Harbin, E. O. (Elvin Oscar), 1885–1955. Fun encyclopedia. III. Title.

GV1201.H383 1983 794 83-2818

ISBN 0-687-27757-4 (v. 4)

0-687-27754-X (v. 1)
0-687-27755-8 (v. 2)
0-687-27756-6 (v. 3)
0-687-27758-2 (v. 5)
0-687-27759-0 (set)

MANUFACTURED BY THE PARTHENON PRESS AT
NASHVILLE, TENNESSEE, UNITED STATES OF AMERICA

CONTENTS

INTRODUCTION

The original *Fun Encyclopedia* by E. O. Harbin presented a fairly comprehensive coverage of the drama and music of that era. Today, however, there are so many more categories in the area of "drama" and so much more available music that it cannot all be incorporated in one book.

Therefore this volume concentrates on materials that can be used by clubs or church groups, at camp, or in the home.

In the first section, I have retained many ideas that can still be used today, and I have added other stunts and skits—some new, some proven—and a section on puppetry.

The music section includes some of today's new action songs and musical games, as well as the old traditional melodies. These old songs are a part of our heritage and should be preserved. Teach them to the younger generation—sing them with the older generation!

Enjoy the skits and the music! Sing and have fun!

1

FUN WITH DRAMA

Drama—A word that in itself stirs the imagination, projecting a variety of methods for communicating a story, a situation, or an idea.

Drama can take any of these forms:

The Play: A play usually is a story acted out in front of an audience to communicate a situation or an idea.

Monologue: In this form of drama an actor may represent one central character, or several. Few or no props are required, and a costume may or may not be needed. Any extensive monologue requires creative acting ability to keep the attention of the audience.

Storytelling: A storyteller has developed the art of painting pictures with words—communicating with the imagination. Those who listen can be caught spellbound by what is being said or read.

Pantomime: Here the actors communicate without the use of words. Facial expressions, body movements, and gestures create a mood, an emotion, an attitude, a deed or an event.

Pantomime and music go hand in hand. One can "lip sync" a song, pretend to play a musical instrument, or, through rhythmic expression, interpret the words or mood of a song, as is done by dancers and figure skaters.

Clowning is a form of mime. Everyone wants to be a clown. And why not? It is an opportunity to be someone else, or just to be yourself behind a funny face. Clowns can visit hospitals and nursing homes and can appear at parties. Wherever there is a clown, there are smiling faces.

Puppetry: In recent years, the rebirth of puppetry has captured the hearts of children, youths, and adults. Messages, announcements, and ideas often can be communicated more effectively with puppets than through any other medium.

A puppet may be in the form of a person, an animal, or any sort of strange creature. A hand puppet can be made from a spoon, a paper plate, a sock, a styrofoam ball, some furry material, a box, or a piece of wood. Marionettes are puppets that are manipulated with strings. They can be small, medium, or large—life-size to giant-size. It requires a great deal of skill and long hours of practice to become an effective puppeteer.

Tableau: This is a simple but effective way to visually portray an idea or thought. The actors remain in fixed positions, like living statues.

A tableau may be combined with music, and a story or other message may be presented. At Christmastime, a nativity scene brings the message of the birth of Christ. Tableau is a good form of drama.

Choral Speaking: A group can relate a message to an audience through various inflections of the voice. At times only one person may speak, at times only females or males, only a few persons, or the entire choir. The material may be memorized or read from a script.

Improvisation: This word applies to unrehearsed role playing—stunts, skits, and simulation/theater games that require minimal preparation.

Pageantry: A pageant is a large spectacular performance to celebrate a historical event or a special theme. Pageants may be performed indoors or out and usually are accompanied by music, have a large cast, and feature special effects.

Street Drama: These organized performances can occur on the street, in a shopping center, on the beach, in a park, at a fair, or just in a neighborhood. The costuming and production should be simple but entertaining.

Reader's Theater: In this oral interpretation, a group of actors read from a script to interpret the message for the audience.

Fun Drama: Stunts and short humorous plays fall into this category and may or may not directly involve the audience. You will find several suggestions for this type of activity in the following pages.

There are many resources in the Bibliography for each of these types of drama.

DRAMATIC GAMES

Charades—A charade is the dramatic presentation of a word so that the audience can guess what the word is. Usually charades are done in pantomime. Sometimes they are acted out with dialogue. They may be simple or elaborate. The players choose a word, phrase, or sentence. Each part has a separate meaning. The audience is told the number of syllables or words in the charade and in how many scenes it will be presented. Then the audience tries to guess the word.

Gestures—This has been called one-person charades, since it combines both pantomime and guessing. It requires only two people—one to gesticulate and the other to guess what the weird movements represent. However, any number of people may play. The players take turns acting out something perplexing for the others to guess: songs, book titles, cars, names, familiar sights, famous sayings, words, and so on.

Dramatic Adverbs—One player leaves the room. The rest select some suitable adverb. The player returns and tries to discover what the word is by asking questions and observing the manner of reply. In answering, each player must act in a manner that suggests the word. For instance, if the word were *sadly,* each response would be made in a doleful manner until the player guesses the word. A player might say, "I am sorry, my dear friend. It grieves me beyond measure that I cannot disclose the word to you." The player who furnishes the last clue leaves the room and the game continues.

Suggested words: sweetly, excitedly, angrily, laughingly, crazily, haltingly.

Dramagrams—Players divide into two teams and choose captains. Each team makes up a list of short quotations, book titles, advertising slogans, proverbs, and the like. The captains exchange lists, and then the fun begins. One player comes up to the team captain, who whispers the first quotation, title, or slogan. That player then tries to convey the phrase to their teammates by acting it out. All acting must be in pantomime. The number of fingers held up indicate the number of words. Some teammate may ask, "Is it a slogan?" The player vigorously shakes head, "No." "Is it a quotation?" Player nods "Yes," then starts acting it out, starting anywhere, but indicating the location of that word by holding up the correct number of fingers. For instance, suppose the quotation is "Give me liberty or give me death." The player holds up seven fingers, then holds up one to indicate the first word and acts out "Give," putting on a begging act. The player then holds up two fingers and points to self, then holds up seven and does a dying act. By this time the teammates will probably have guessed the quotation. If not, the player acts out the other words, trying to tell them what the quotation is.

Hunter, Fox, and Gun—Two lines of players stand facing each other. The players in each line consult to determine whether their team will be the hunter, the gun, or the fox. To save the necessity of consultation each time, they may decide what they will be for three successive times. They should be sure that everyone in the line thoroughly understands. At the same time they are careful to keep the secret from the other side. The leader counts "One, two, three!" On "three," each side begins to perform. For instance, if one side has decided on hunter, each player in that line poses with one foot forward, shading eyes with right hand, at the same time saying, "Aha," three times. The "guns" stand as if aiming with a rifle and shout "Bang!" The "foxes" put thumbs in their ears, wiggle their fingers, and bark with a sharp "Yip, yip, yip!"

Scoring is done on the following basis: "Fox" beats the "hunter," "hunter" beats the "gun," and "gun" beats the "fox."

Grab-Bag Drama—Divide into groups. Each group is provided with a bag full of items to use in working out a skit. Allow five to ten minutes for preparing this impromptu activity. Suggestions for the grab bags:

Baseball cap	Indian headdress
Umbrella	Candle
Ladies hat	Dog collar and leash
Paintbrush	Bow tie
Barbell	Hair ribbon
Empty soft-drink bottle	Water pistol

Miss Paper America Pageant—Divide into groups of five. Each group selects a candidate for Miss America. With newspaper, construction paper, crepe paper, tape, pins, and so on, each group creates a costume to be judged. The candidates may wear banners such as: Miss Cellaneous, Miss Take, Miss Understood, Miss Fortune.

Miss A*male*ica—Divide into groups. Each group chooses a male candidate for this beauty pageant. Each contestant is to compete in swim suit, talent, and evening gown competition—keep it in good taste and proper perspective. The judges pick contestants for first, second, and third place. The winner can be crowned with a glittered cardboard crown and presented with some dead flowers. Photographs will keep this event fresh in everyone's memory.

Bride and Groom—A wedding shower for couples will be enhanced by this fun stunt. The male guests are given white tissue paper and tape or pins. They are to dress the bride in a creative wedding dress. The female guests are given the same materials to dress the groom. The couple then model their wedding attire.

Hair Stylist—Ask for four male volunteers. Have them sit facing the group. Then select four females and blindfold them. Place protective coverings (shower curtains or pieces of plastic) around the males. With a can of shaving cream, each female is to create a hair style for her candidate. The group votes for the best style. Provide towels for the messy cleanup.

Feed the Baby—Fill baby bottles with milk or soft drink and place a baby's bonnet on the head of each male contestant. Females from the group serve as mommies for the babies. The winner is the team that finishes its bottle first.

Variation: Place bibs and blindfolds on all players, and let mommies try to feed the babies chocolate pudding.

Blind Feeding the Blind—Blindfold two players. Furnish them with spoons and powdered sugar or ice cream or shelled peanuts. They sit facing each other, and each tries to feed the other. Protect the floor with newspapers and the players by tying aprons or towels about their necks.

STUNTS AND SKITS

Whether at a party, at camp, at home, at school, at a club meeting or banquet, or in an assembly program, fun drama is appropriate. It can be in the form of a stunt, a prepared "mellerdramer" or other skit, and it can also include members of the audience. There is a major difference between a skit and a stunt: A skit has a prepared script and has been rehearsed; a stunt is spontaneous activity.

Here are some guidelines:

1. Be sure the skit or stunt is appropriate for the age group.
2. All skits and stunts should be in good taste.

3. Know your material well and be prepared for any emergency situations that might occur.
4. Be sure the audience can see and hear.
5. When there is to be audience participation, give adequate, clear instructions. If necessary, demonstrate.
6. Make the experience fun for both those who participate and those who watch. Do not drag out the activity to the point that it becomes tiresome.
7. Be enthusiastic! Enjoy the following stunts and skits!

The Lost Sheep—The leader makes an elaborate announcement to introduce a soloist who is to sing a pathetic ballad titled "The Lost Sheep." The singer takes a position at front, glances at the accompanist, signals the pianist to begin, stands ready as the prelude is played, and then gives a plaintive "Baa-aa-aa."

A Dream Song—In a camp, conference, or group where there is a notorious snorer, this stunt goes over well. The perpetrator announces a new song, composed by the aforesaid snorer, entitled "A Dream Song." The person who is to sing the composition then stands up and snores loudly.

The Giant Sneeze—Divide the crowd into three sections. At a signal, Section One is to shout "Ka-hishi," Section Two, "Ka-hashi," and Section Three, "Ka-hoshoo." "All together! One-two-three! Go!"

A Fake Argument—At an appropriate time during a banquet, stunt program, or party, someone rises to protest some statement that has been made or some feature of the program. Other "instructed" persons take sides in the ensuing argument, with the intention of drawing someone into it who does not know that it is a stunt. When the argument has waxed warm, one of the perpetrators rises and thanks the crowd for helping in their stunt.

Boots Without Shoes—Victims are called in one at a time. The leader goes through various gyrations as the victim is commanded to say "Boots without shoes." The luckless individual will probably try valiantly to imitate the leader in saying, "Boots without shoes." But the leader says, "No, you are wrong. Say it the way I tell you: 'Boots without shoes.' " The victim again tries to imitate the gestures and voice inflections of the leader, but again it is wrong. Finally, it dawns on the victim that the way to say "Boots without shoes" is simply to say "Boots."

The Moon Is Big and Round—The leader stands before a group of players and repeats, "The moon is big and round. It has two eyes, a nose, and a mouth," making a sweeping circle with the left hand to indicate that the moon is "big and round." For the "two eyes" and "nose," dots are made with the forefinger; for the "mouth," a small semicircular motion. The leader then invites others in the group to do the same thing. Most of them will fail and wonder why. They will try to imitate the leader's voice inflection, stance, and motions. A few may get it right. The secret, of course, is that the leader makes the motions with the left hand. Most persons will use the right hand.

Joining the Sack Society—The players are brought in one at a time and, with one eye closed, are required to thread a needle. Be sure to use a needle with a large eye to make the threading a simple matter. The leader makes sure each player has closed an eye by putting a hand over it. The catch is that there is soot or greasepaint on the hand, and thus the candidate is given a black eye. Immediately after the threading is finished, the leader explains that all members must don the society regalia. This is a large paper sack that fits over the head. It has two small holes for the eyes and may have other features marked on it. All members of the society, including the leader, are wearing these sacks. This procedure prevents subsequent victims from discovering the trick. After all the new members have been initiated, suggest that everyone now remove the headgear. The looks of surprise when the black eyes are disclosed will be laughable.

Rubber-band Nose Twister—Place a rubber band around the head and nose of each participant. The first to get the rubber band off the nose wins.

Mesmerism—Announce that a certain person in the group has special hypnotic powers. Ask for volunteers and select one to be a subject.

The hypnotist and the victim face each other. The subject is told to look the hypnotist squarely in the eye and do just what the hypnotist does, using as nearly as possible the same tone of voice and making the same motions. A saucer is handed to the hypnotist, and another is handed to the subject. The hypnotist says,

> "Ready? Now, after me:
> I touch my saucer's underside,
> And then I let my finger glide
> Across my forehead, down my nose,
> Touch my chin and cheeks of rose;
> And after I have done this much,
> My saucer's inside then I touch."

Now give a mirror to the victim, who will see that the face in the mirror is streaked with soot or greasepaint, which had been smeared on the underside of the saucer.

Dime Press—Ask for a volunteer for this stunt. Say that you are going to press a dime upon the volunteer's forehead. Allow the volunteer to touch the dime to see that there is no adhesive on it. Then say that after the dime has been pressed upon the forehead, the volunteer is to try to shake it off without touching it.

The idea is that after you press the dime firmly to the forehead for a couple of minutes and then remove it, the forehead will feel as though the dime were still there.

The Water Stunt—If possible, rig up an old-fashioned well on the stage. Or on top of a table place a bucket which presumably holds water drawn from a well. In fact, it holds only a large dipper containing a bit of water. Several people come on stage and observe the well. One remarks about the good water. Person Two professes to be thirsty and lifts the dipper. Tasting the water, Two spits it out and dashes the rest of the contents of the dipper on the floor.

"This water is terrible," Two says, picks up the bucket, and pretends to throw water right at the audience. There is a swish, screams, and ducking, and then some sheepish grins. The bucket contained some rice. As it leaves the bucket it sounds and looks like water.

Something Never Seen Before—Announce that you plan to show something that has never been seen before and never will be seen again. Then produce a peanut or thin-s)elled pecan. Crack the shell and display the nut inside. Explain that this is something that has never been seen before this very moment. Then eat the nut and announce, "And it will never be seen again."

Fake Pillow Fight—Two players are blindfolded. Each is provided with a pillow. They start toward each other from opposite sides of the room. The object is to see who can score the most hits. Unknown to the blindfolded players, the referee also is furnished with a pillow and hits first one and then the other player. Each player thinks the opponent is doing the hitting.

Knot-Tying Trick—Provide a piece of rope or string, or use a handkerchief. Ask if anyone can tie a knot in the rope by taking hold of both ends and not letting go with either hand. After they have tried, demonstrate how it can be done. Fold the arms, the left hand under the right elbow and the right hand over the left elbow. In this position take hold of the ends of the rope. Now unfold the arms without letting go of the ends, and the knot is tied.

Strong Man—Ask for volunteers who think they can lift a four-legged wooden chair by grasping a leg with one hand. This is almost impossible.

Balanced Writing—If you think you have a good sense of balance try this one. Stand a gallon jug upright. Sit down on it and cross your legs, touching the floor only with the heel of one foot. In this position, hold a pad in your hand and try to write your name. Or hold a candle, strike a match, and light the candle. Or try threading a needle from this position.

Pat Head and Rub Stomach—Try to pat your head with one hand and rub your stomach with the other, simultaneously.

Move If You Can—Stand with one side (hip, shoulder, and head) against a wall. Now try to lift the free leg sideways without changing your position.

Arise—Lie flat on your back, arms to the side, hands flat against your thighs. In this position, try to rise without using your hands. First come to a sitting position and then stand, if you can.

Rise with Arms Crossed—Lie flat on your back, arms crossed on your chest. Try to rise without uncrossing your arms or using your elbows.

Pick It Up—Stand with your back against a wall, heels touching the wall. Try to pick up a coin without moving your heels away from the wall. You deserve the coin if you can perform this trick.

Kneeling—Stand with your toes on a line. Without using your hands or moving your feet, kneel down and get up again.

Circle Two—Try moving both arms in a circle (rotary motion) in opposite directions, the right hand away from the body and the left toward the body.

Blowing Out the Candle—A player is blindfolded, moved back three steps, turned around, and permitted to take three steps before attempting to blow out a candle which rests on a table. If you think this is easy, try it.

Peanut Butter—For best results while performing this stunt, speak with tip of your tongue touching the roof of your mouth. Suggested monologue:

There are three ways to get peanut butter off the roof of your mouth. One way is to swallow it. *(Swallow hard, making the pantomime bold enough to be seen by everybody.)* But that doesn't always work.

Another way to get peanut butter out of your mouth is to blow it out. *(Pantomime this action in exaggerated manner.)* But that doesn't always work.

The other way is to scrape it out with your finger. *(Laboriously scrape it out and hold it up on the end of your finger. Then talk in a normal voice.)*

There are three ways to get peanut butter off the end of your finger. One way is to blow it off. *(Make a real effort to blow it off.)* But that doesn't always work.

Another way to get peanut butter off your finger is to shake it off. *(Try desperately to shake the peanut butter off. Some of it flies off and lands on your clothes.)* But that is too messy. *(Wipe off the side of your leg.)*

The other way to get peanut butter off your finger is to lick it off. *(Place finger back in your mouth and lick the peanut butter off. Now you're back where you started with your mouth full again.)*

Now, there are three ways to get peanut butter off the roof of your mouth.

Bluebeard Lock and Key—Players are taken into another room and given a chance to unlock Bluebeard's lock. A key is provided, and the person inserts it in the lock. But does it unlock? It does not. With a howl, the player lets go of the key in a hurry. The lock has been connected to a battery. When the key is inserted, someone throws the switch and the electricity does the rest.

Halloween Stunt—In coming out of one room, the guests are required to step down into another room, which is dark. As they step down they land on a set of bed springs, covered with a piece of carpet. If both rooms are on the same level, fix a step so they will have to come down on the springs from an elevation. Tiny ghosts painted with phosphorescent paint can flit across the room. This can be done by stretching a wire across the room, one end higher than the other. The ghosts can be attached to bent pins and placed on the wire. They'll slide across as if they were flying through space. There may also be a skeleton or two moving about. Skeleton masks and dark suits covered with strips of cloth painted with phosphorescent paint will do the work here. A person standing in a dark corner with a lighted flashlight held just below the chin looks very weird.

Polly Wolly Beanbag—Enlist a few volunteers who are new to your group. Explain to them that you are initiating them into an exclusive club—the Polly Wolly Beanbag Club. Send the volunteers out of the room. Place two chairs so that their sides face the audience. The leader dresses in any type of ridiculous clothing, to look like a grand master of some lodge. The first volunteer is ushered into the room and sits in the seat of honor. The leader sits in the other chair and instructs the new member to stand when the leader stands, sit when the leader sits, and to repeat "Polly Wolly Beanbag" after the leader, and in the same manner (fast, slow).

The leader stands and sits several times, saying "Polly Wolly Beanbag." The new inductee follows suit. Sometime during this ceremony, while the inductee is standing, a person behind the inductee's chair slips a wet sponge into the seat. When the leader sits down, the inductee sits on a wet sponge.

After all the inductees have been "initiated," each may receive a hand-written certificate for completing the ceremony.

Knight of the Whistle—Several players who do not know this stunt are sent out of the room and recalled one at a time. On entering the room, the candidate is presented to the High Commander of the Order of Knight of the Silver Whistle. The Commander explains that the candidate, to be proved worthy of the honor about to be bestowed, will be blindfolded while one of the Knights hides the insignia of the Order, a silver whistle. This the candidate must find. On finding it, the candidate will be received into full membership.

The candidate is taken to the center of the room to be blindfolded. As the others crowd around, the whistle, attached to a piece of string, is fastened to the candidate's back. Then the blindfold is removed and the hunt proceeds. At intervals, when the candidate's back is turned, players blow the whistle. The candidate will turn swiftly, but cannot locate the whistle. This goes on until the hoax is discovered. Then the candidate is made a full-fledged Knight and another candidate is ushered into the room.

The Court of Love—Certain members of the group should be brought before the court on charges of having broken the laws of Sweetheart Land. The King should render decisions on cases that concern the ladies of the court, while the Queen rules on cases that involve the knights. Have this part of the program well planned. Pick out well-known "knights" and "ladies" for trial. The prosecutor should name the culprit and the offense. The defendant has an opportunity to answer the charges if desired. A knight may be charged with breaking the laws of the kingdom by remaining impervious, hard-hearted, and unmoved by the charms of the ladies of the kingdom. Or he may be charged with scattering his affections and refusing to concentrate them, thus breaking one of the oldest laws of the kingdom. A lady of the court may be charged with cold-blooded heart breaking.

Balloon Tune—Select four volunteers to be your balloon orchestra. Give each a balloon to inflate. The neck of an inflated balloon can be stretched to create a squeaking noise. Have the piano play and/or the group can sing, "la-la-la," the tune of "Blue Danube." Each time they reach a specific spot in the melody, the balloon accompanists should squeak. Example: La, la, la-la-la, squeak-squeak, squeak-squeak, and so on, until the music creates quite a sensation.

Wash the Elephant—Wash an elephant? It can be done, and it is hilarious. Send three or four volunteers out of the room. Explain to the remaining group that you are going to pantomime washing an elephant; indicate the position of the head. When the first volunteer returns, explain that you are going to pantomime an action. Tell the person to concentrate and watch your movements closely, since each volunteer must illustrate the same pantomime for the next volunteer.

Walk to the space where the "elephant" is supposed to be standing. Survey the elephant by looking up toward the top of his back. Walk over to a wall, pantomime picking up a bucket. Turn on a "faucet," watch the bucket fill with "water," and turn the faucet off. Pick up the bucket and a "brush" with a long handle and walk over to the elephant.

Dip the brush into the bucket and begin to wash one side—scrub under the elephant's stomach, lift up the large ear, wash behind it, then scrub it inside with a circular motion. Walk around the front of the elephant and wash the other side. This time, scrub the back (stand on tiptoe). Clean the other ear.

Walk to the front of the elephant and scrub the trunk. Lift the trunk in order to brush the teeth and tusks. Each time you scrub a portion of the elephant, dip the brush in the bucket. When you have finished scrubbing, return to the faucet and lay down the brush and bucket. Pantomime putting a hose on the faucet, turn it on, and spray the elephant all over—remember to lift the ears and spray behind them and inside in a circular motion. Then walk over to the faucet and turn it off.

Now tell the first volunteer to repeat the instructions and the pantomime for volunteer Number Two. When Number One finishes, Number Two calls in Number Three and repeats the process. When all have finished, ask the volunteers what they thought they were doing. Then tell them they were washing an elephant.

Make It Rain—Divide the group into three smaller groups. When everyone is seated, explain that they must maintain complete silence for this skit. They are to listen closely and use their imaginations. Tell them you will not be saying anything, but when you face each group, they are to repeat the motion and sound you make.

Face group one. Place your palms together and rub them back and forth, making a sound like wind. Turn and do the same for group two, then group three. When all three groups are rubbing their palms together, turn back to group one and begin to snap your fingers—first on the right hand, then the left. Turn and do the same for group two, then group three. When everyone is snapping fingers, turn to group one and stop snapping your fingers; begin to pat your thighs with your hands, alternating your right and left hands. Do this for groups two and three. Then return to group one and begin stamping your feet, first the right, then the left. Stamp relatively fast. Do the same with groups two and three.

Now begin to reverse the action by turning to group one and patting your thighs. Do the same for groups two and three. Then turn to group one and snap your fingers. Do this for groups two and three. Turn to group one and begin rubbing your palms together. Do the same for groups two and three. Then stop group one, then groups two and three.

Between each action, allow enough time for the players to imagine they hear rain falling.

Whistle the Three Bears—Select four people to play the parts, and ask them to act out the story of "The Three Bears," using various whistle tones instead of words. This will require a little practice.

The Echo—This stunt is usually done indoors. Tell everyone they must really concentrate on hearing the echo.

Begin by calling out, "Howdy." After a second or two, someone hidden offstage or in another room responds with "Howdy." Next shout out that one of the girls is pretty: "Robin Roberts is really beautiful." The echo responds appropriately. Then call out a boy's name: "Keith Chafin is the handsomest guy here." Wait for a response. The echo does not respond. Shout it out again and wait. The echo finally responds, "Baloney!"

Shadow Pictures—Use the shadow-picture idea for some interesting stunts. Suggestions:

Operation: Have a victim on the table. Use a saw, big knife, hatchet, a bicycle pump for thermometer, etc. Take out a string of sausages, a can, a cabbage, a toy dog, and other things. Pretend to operate on the patient's head. Have the patient scream as you cut into a cabbage, making a sickening sound.

Beauty Parlor: Use ridiculous looking instruments. Appear to form the hair into unusual shapes.

Dentist Chair: Use coal tongs for forceps. Draw out a gigantic tooth.

The Sentimentalist Club—People from the audience are invited to join the Sentimentalist Club. They are brought in one at a time. The leader instructs the candidate that all questions must be answered truthfully and may put each one through some sort of intelligence test, asking, "How many eggs in a dozen?" and several other such questions. Then suddenly the initiator commands: "Say, 'Whom you love.' " The victim may respond facetiously. Members of the club will protest with "I object!" The leader will explain that the candidate will please not try to be funny, and again commands, "Say, 'Whom you love.' " The victim will respond with some name. Again the members shout, "I object! The candidate is not answering correctly." Each time the candidate answers with some name, the members shout, "Objection." The initiator may give the victim some clues by suggesting, "Say, 'I have cold feet' " or "Say, 'I have a soft head.' " After a while the answer dawns, the candidate repeats "Whom you love," and all the members applaud. The candidate is now a full-fledged member. (Care must be taken not to unduly embarrass any who are timid or sensitive.)

The Barnyard Club—Candidates for election to the Barnyard Club are brought in one by one. They are duly impressed with the importance of membership. "Every candidate must pass certain tests before admission to membership," explains the leader. "Face me and do as I tell you." The candidate faces the leader. There is a vacant chair immediately behind the victim. "In order to qualify for membership," says the leader, "you must imitate some animal of the barnyard, suggested by the group and satisfactory to the group." He then turns to the members and asks, "What animal shall it be?" "A hog," shouts someone. A chorus of voices protest "No! No! That is too personal!" "A donkey!" shouts another. Again there come protests on the ground that this suggestion not only is too personal but that it is unfair to the donkey. Other animals may be mentioned. When someone finally calls, "A hen!" everyone agrees to that.

"All right," says the leader to the candidate, "cluck like a hen that has just laid an egg." As the candidate clucks, someone slips a hard-boiled egg into the chair. The leader asks the candidate to turn around and look at the chair, then announces, "You have qualified. We recognize you as a full-fledged member of the Barnyard Club."

Bow to the King of Siam—Ask some people from the audience to come to the front of the room. Have the King of Siam (dressed in robe and crown) walk to a throne and sit down. The volunteers are to walk up to the king, kneel, and say several times—very slowly at first but faster each time: "O wa ta goo Siam." Or you can have them all sing these words to the tune of "America":

O wa ta goo
O wa ta goo
O wa ta goo Siam
O wa ta goo
O wa ta goo
O wa ta goo Siam

Soon they will realize they are saying, "Oh what a goose I am."

The Burial of Old Man Kant—Participants can hum a mournful tune, or if there is a piano, someone can play a funeral dirge. Enter five people, one leading the way, the other four carrying a coffin about two feet long, made of black cardboard. On it is written in big white letters, OLD MAN KANT. This is carried to a platform or to the front of the room and placed on the floor. The person who led the way then proceeds to perform the burial ceremony. "I come not to praise Old Man Kant, but to bury him. He is an old and ornery member of this group. He has made himself felt in all our activities through these many years. We consign his body to the grave, with the hope that he shall never be resurrected. Dust to dust and ashes to ashes! May he never suffer from the cold where he is going."

The pallbearers weep bitter tears, wringing the water out of wet sponges which they have hidden inside their handkerchiefs.

Immediately following this ceremony, someone rises and says, "We have just buried Old Man Kant. We now wish to present our new emblem and motto." With these words the person holds up a new tin can with large letters WE and shouts, "WE CAN."

Trip to Mexico—Select three or four volunteers from the group and have them come up front and stand side by side. Explain to them that you are going to tell a story to the audience. When you finish the first part of the story, the person beside you is to repeat the same story and the same motion. Then the next person does the same—repeats the story and the motion. All the motions are to be continued throughout the entire story.

Begin the story: "I had never been to Mexico, so when I was in Texas last year, I decided to drive down. As I came to the border, the guard stopped me. I said, 'Sir, I would like to visit your country.' He replied, 'Señor, you must cut a lot of red tape in order to get into Mexico.' So I reached into my pocket *(put right hand in pocket),* pulled out my scissors *(pull hand out of pocket),* and cut the red tape *(with first two fingers of right hand, pretend to cut; continue cutting throughout the skit)."*

Nod for the person next to you to begin. Do not prompt the volunteers unless they get too far off the track. When the last person has finished the skit and is pretending to cut, begin the second part.

"After I cut the red tape, I asked the guard if I could enter the country. He said, 'Si, you may go in.' " Nod your head up and down and continue throughout the rest of the skit. The next person is to repeat the words and the motion. When the last person has finished the skit and is nodding, begin the next part.

"After he said I could go in, I waved goodbye to him." With left hand, wave goodbye. The others are to repeat the words and action. When the last person has finished the skit and is waving, begin the next part.

"I arrived at the motel and checked in. After I entered the elevator, it broke down and we kept going up and down." Do half squats by bending and straightening your knees. By now you should be cutting with your right hand, nodding your head, waving goodbye with your left hand, and doing knee bends. When the last person is doing all this, continue with the next part.

"On the elevator there was a woman with a box. In the box she had a white rat. It got out and I began to stamp on it." Between knee bends, stamp the floor with your right foot. When the last person is stamping, go to the last part.

"There was another lady on the elevator. She had a cuckoo clock. It began to cuckoo and wouldn't stop. It went, 'Cuckoo! Cuckoo!' " Keep saying "Cuckoo" over and over. Between "Cuckoos," stick out your tongue as if it were the cuckoo on a clock. After the last person has finished, the group deserves a round of applause.

Fun with a Pillowcase—With felt-tip markers, draw large eyes, nose, and mouth for a funny or scary creature on a white pillowcase. The entire case serves as the head of the creature.

Place the pillowcase over a person's head and shoulders. The person's hands should be placed on the head with the elbows sticking out, so that the pillowcase will stand straight out. Be sure the face is straight on the body of the person. Next, place a cardigan sweater around the waist of the person and fasten all the buttons. Stuff the arms of the sweater with paper and place gloves where the hands should be. White gloves are most effective.

A group of these creatures can march into a room and do a dance number, sing, perform a skit, or put on a fashion show.

The Dancing Midgets—Two or more of these midgets could be arranged by taking an old sheet and cutting holes for the head, legs, and arms. Pin tiny costumes on the outside of the sheet. The head of one person appears in the large hole in the sheet and this person's hands and arms (on which have been placed baby shoes and stockings) appear in the two holes cut for the midget's legs. A second person stands behind the first. The second person's arms are placed under the first person's armpits and through the arm holes, thus providing the midget's hands. A table is provided on which the midgets can dance. They may also talk, sing, or put on a skit. A bit of imagination will disclose the possibilities in this stunt.

From *The New Fun Encyclopedia,* Vol. 2, *Parties and Banquets,* p. 50.

Stagecoach—Players stand or sit in a circle and number off by sevens. All 1s become cowboys; all 2s, Indians; all 3s, women; all 4s, horses; all 5s, stagecoaches; all 6s, rifles; and all 7s, bows and arrows.

The leader reads a story about the holdup of a stage. When the "cowboys" are mentioned, they pretend to be driving a stage at a furious pace and shout, "Yip! Yip!" The "Indians" war dance and yell. The "women" scream. The "horses" beat a tattoo on the floor with their feet, or on their knees with their hands. The "stagecoaches" turn completely around. The "rifles" take aim and shout "Bang!" The "bows and arrows" drop to one knee or stand, draw their bows, and shout "Zip!" It would be well to practice once before proceeding.

Suggested story:

> It was in the days of *stagecoaches* and *cowboys* and *Indians*. Alkali Ike, Dippy Dick, and Pony Pete were three courageous *cowboys*. When the *stagecoach* left for Rainbow's End they were aboard, as were two *women*, Salty Sal and Frosty Flo. The *stagecoach* was drawn by three handsome *horses*, and it left Dead End exactly on time.
>
> The most dangerous part of the journey was the pass known as Gory Gulch. As the *stagecoach* neared this spot, the *women* were a bit nervous and the *cowboys* were alert, fingering their *rifles* as if ready for any emergency. Even the *horses* seemed to sense danger.
>
> Sure enough, just as the *stagecoach* entered the Gulch, there sounded the blood-curdling war whoop of the *Indians*. Mounted on *horses*, they came riding wildly toward the *stagecoach*, aiming their *bows and arrows*. The *cowboys* took aim with their *rifles* and fired. The *women* screamed. The *horses* pranced nervously. The *Indians* shot their *bows and arrows*. The *cowboys* fired their *rifles* again, this time with more deadly effect. The leading brave fell, and the *Indians* turned their *horses* and fled, leaving their *bows and arrows* behind. The *women* fainted. The *cowboys* shot once more with their *rifles*, just for luck. The driver urged the *horses* on, and the *stagecoach* sped down the trail.

From *The New Fun Encyclopedia*, Vol. 2, *Parties and Banquets*, pp. 75-76.

Drama in Three Speeds—Choose five males from the audience to play the parts of King, Queen, Princess, Prince, and Page. Select those to whom the audience will respond with enthusiasm. Dress the King in robe (sheet) and crown (cardboard). Hand him the royal scepter (rolled-up newspaper) and seat him on the throne (chair). Place a robe (sheet) and wig and crown (paper) on the Queen and have him sit on a throne (chair) next to the King. The next character is the beautiful Princess. Dress him in a robe (sheet), wig and crown (paper), and have him stand next to the Queen. The handsome Prince is next, wearing a cape and hunting hat. A sword may be hung around his waist. The Page is dressed in a cap.

Explain to the audience that this is a rehearsal. As the action begins, the Prince and Page are standing off-stage, away from the royal family. The Page walks in, kneels in front of the King, and says, "Oh, King, there is a man without." The King replies, "Without what?" The Page responds, "Without the gate." The King answers, "Give him the gate and show him in."

The Page walks to the Prince, and they return. As the Prince enters the presence of the royal family, he looks at the Princess and gives a loud sigh. The Princess responds with "Ooooooh!" The Prince and Page walk over to the King, kneel down, and the Prince says, "Oh, King, I would have the hand of your lovely daughter." The Queen stands up and responds loudly. "Not my daughter!"

The King rises and furiously declares, "Outrageous!" He proceeds to (softly) tap the Queen, the Princess, the Prince, the Page, and then himself on the head. They all fall over as if knocked out.

Announce to the audience that now Act One will be performed in slow motion. Both words and actions are to be done very slowly. After Act One, announce that Act Two will be performed at super speed. The actors are to move and speak as quickly as possible.

Waiting for a Date—If you think this pantomime needs an explanation, tell the audience that you are going to a certain street corner to meet your date.

Begin by walking up to an imaginary street corner. Stop and look up and down the street. Look at your watch. Cross your arms and pat your foot. Then give the impression that you suddenly have had an idea.

Reach into your pocket and pretend to pull out a piece of bubble gum. Unwrap the gum, place in your mouth, and chew. Reach into your pocket and pull out another piece; unwrap it, place it in your mouth, and chew. Repeat this action three or four times. It should seem that you have a huge wad of bubble gum in your mouth as you struggle to chew.

Begin to blow a bubble. As you blow, indicate the size with your hands. When the bubble gets as big as a basketball, pretend that it bursts. It now covers your face. As you would if this really happened, take the gum from your mouth and pretend to unstick it from your face.

When your face is clean, pretend to lean against a light pole. Blow another bubble, again indicating its size with your hands. This bubble grows to the size of three basketballs. Pretend to remove the gum from your mouth, toss the bubble lightly into the air and catch it. Pantomime this several times, wearing a great big smile. Then bounce the bubble like a basketball several times, pick it up, burst it, and put the gum back in your mouth. Be sure to lick your fingers.

Look at your watch again; look up and down the street. Chew slowly on your bubble gum as if you were getting tired of it. But when you take it from your mouth and try to throw it away, it sticks to your hand. As you vigorously sling it, it gets caught in your hair. After a struggle, you get it out of your hair, but then you get it on your clothes. Another struggle to pull it free.

When the bubble gum is finally removed from your clothes, you decide to step on it in order to get it off your hand. You are successful. Then you look up to see your date coming down the street. You wave and smile, but as you step out, you find the gum has stuck your shoe to the ground. You can't move your foot. Your date arrives, you smile sheepishly, shrug your shoulders, and point to your foot.

With a deep sigh, you take your foot out of your shoe and, after a struggle, free the shoe from the ground. Now you pretend to get the gum off the sole by placing it to your face as if you were stuffing the gum back into your mouth. With gum in mouth, shoe back on foot, extend your arm to your date and walk off.

Honeybee—This skit must be prearranged and rehearsed, but the audience must think it is spontaneous. And those involved must be good sports.

The leader (the Honeybee) chooses the prearranged volunteer, the Queen Bee, from the audience.

The Honeybee then gives the Queen Bee instructions: "I am the Honeybee and I am going out into the audience, which is a field of *beautiful* flowers, to gather honey. When I return, I will hit my hand with my fist *(demonstrates)* and say, 'Ummm!' You are to hit your hand with your fist and say, 'Ummm!' " *(Queen Bee does it.)* "I'll go out a second time, return, hit my hand with my fist twice *(demonstrates)* and say, 'Ummm! Ummm!' " *(Queen Bee responds.)* "I'll go out a third time, return, hit my hand with my fist three times, and say, 'Ummm! Ummm! Ummm!' Then *you* are to say, 'Give it all to me, honey!' "

The Honeybee tucks thumbs under armpits, flaps arms up and down, and buzzes or hums like a bee in flight.

Honeybee picks out cute children, nuzzles their necks, and very loudly hums, "Ummm!"; may go to an older man (a good sport) and leave with a sour "Ummm!" Honeybee then returns to the Queen Bee, hits hand with fist once, and says, "Ummm!" The Queen Bee responds with the same action. The Honeybee returns to the audience to gather more honey, returns to the Queen Bee, hits hand with fist twice, and says, "Ummm! Ummm!" The Queen Bee responds. The third time out, after gathering honey, Honeybee goes to a predetermined location where there is hidden a glass of water, takes a mouthful, returns to the Queen Bee, hits hand three times with fist, and says, "Ummm! Ummm! Ummm!" The Queen Bee replies, "Give it all to me, honey!" and the Honeybee sprays the Queen Bee with water.

As audience laughs, the third member of the cast enters the room *obviously*. The wet Queen Bee dries off and asks this prearranged volunteer to come up on stage. The Queen Bee now becomes the Honeybee and explains the process to the new Queen Bee. They rehearse, then go through the actions until the third sequence. While the new Honeybee is getting a mouthful of water, the new Queen Bee is getting a mouthful from a glass hidden on stage.

The Honeybee returns to the Queen Bee, hits hand with fist three times, and says, "Ummm! Ummm! Ummm!" The Queen Bee responds by repeating the same action. Frustrated, the Honeybee shakes head no, repeats the action with a louder, angrier "Ummm! Ummm! Ummm!" while hitting hand with fist harder. The Queen again responds, also louder and angrier. After a third try, the Honeybee swallows the water and says, "You are supposed to say, 'Give it all to me, honey,' " at which the new Queen Bee sprays the new Honeybee with water.

Paying the Rent—The leader of a small group could present this stunt first. Then everyone could do it in unison. Repeat the lines in rhythm. All right, everybody! Let's go!

Landlord (deep growling voice; hold tissue or napkin to upper lip for mustache): I've come for the rent! I've come for the rent!
Heroine (falsetto voice in distress; hold tissue or napkin to side of head like a hair bow): But I can't pay the rent! I can't pay the rent!
Landlord: You must pay the rent! You must pay the rent!
Heroine: Oh, who will pay the rent? Who will pay the rent?
Hero (manly voice; hold napkin to neck like bow tie): I'll pay the rent! I'll pay the rent!
Heroine: My hero! My hero!
Landlord: Curses! Curses!

A Russian Drama—An announcer makes an elaborate introduction, expounding the merits of Russian drama and mentioning names of writers like Chekhov, Dostoevsky, Tolstoy.

CAST

I. Strutsky, the hero (wears bathrobe and bandage around head; has face whitened; evidently does not feel well)

Ima Bugsky, the heroine (looks as ridiculous as possible; seems stupid, never changes expression)

ACT I

(Strutsky sits on stage with feet in pan of water; groans as if in misery.)

Ima Bugsky (stands in foreground, licking lollipop; speaks solemnly): The hero is sick.

ACT II

Ima Bugsky (again speaks solemnly): The hero is very, very sick.

ACT III

Ima Bugsky: The hero is so sick we cannot give the show.

CURTAIN

The Poor Little Match Girl—The parts are all played by one person, who indicates a change in character by changing headgear.

CAST

The Little Match Girl (player puts scarf on head)
The Villain (player pulls cap down over eyes and looks tough)
The Hero (player puts on man's hat and smiles)

(Scene opens with Match Girl shivering in the cold. She has a handful of torn paper and tosses it in the air to indicate it is snowing.)

Girl: Oh, who will help me? Who will help me? I am so cold (br-r-r-r) and I am starving. Who will help me?
Villain: I'll help you, kid.
Girl: Oh, you will help me?
Villain: Yeh, I'll help you.
Girl: How will you help me?
Villain: I will marry you. That's how I will help you.
Girl (frightened): Oh, you will marry me?
Villain: Yeh, I'll marry you.
Girl: But I don't want to marry you. Oh, who will help me? Who will help me? I'm so cold (br-r-r-r).
Hero: I will help you, madam.
Girl (pleased): Oh, you will help me? How will you help me?
Hero: I will marry you.

Girl (evidently delighted): Oh, you will marry me?
Hero: Yes, I will marry you.
Villain: You will not marry her.
Hero: I will marry her.
Villain: I say you will not marry her.
Hero: And why will I not marry her?
Girl: Yes, why won't he marry me?
Villain: Because her father is a spy in the mint.
Hero (looks dejected): What, her father is a spy in the mint?
Girl: Oh! Oh! Oh! Woe is me! Woe is me! My father is a mint spy (mince pie).

CURTAIN

The Crooked Mouth Family—Play takes place in a small-town store.

CAST

Ma (speaks throughout with upper lip extended over lower lip)
Pa (speaks throughout with lower lip extended over upper lip)
Sue, the daughter (speaks out of left side of mouth)
Zeke, the customer (speaks out of right side of mouth)

(Play opens with Pa and Ma puttering around in the store. Pa snaps finger.)

Ma (looks his way inquiringly): What's the matter, Pa? Fergit something?
Pa: Sure did. Fergot to stop by Lem Jones' house to get that five dozen eggs he has for me. Guess I'll have to go back. (He gets his coat and hat and leaves.)
Ma (calls after him): Don't get any more of that rancid butter from him!
Sue (enters languidly, nibbling on a cracker): Hullo, Ma. Where's Pa?

Ma: He's gone down to Lem Jones' to get them eggs. Now that you're here, I'll go on back to the house and get my washing together. You take care of the store.

Sue: Aw, Ma!

(Ma leaves. Customer enters.)

Sue (perking up): Anything I can do for you?

Customer: Yes. I want a box of matches.

Sue (indignant): You quit making fun of me!

Customer (surprised): I'm not making fun of you.

Sue (begins to cry): Ma! There's a man out here making fun of me.

Ma (steps in and glares at customer): What do you mean, making fun of my daughter?

Customer: I'm not making fun of her. I talk this way all the time.

Ma: That's all right, then. Susie, get the man what he wants.

(Sue waits on the customer. He holds her hand as she hands him the matches.)

Customer: Say, I like you! Why can't we get married?

Sue (excited): Ma! This man wants to marry me!

Ma (indifferently): Wal, why not?

Sue (turning to customer): All right, mister. I'll marry you—what's your name? Let's go get married now. (They leave arm in arm.)

(Pa returns. Takes off coat and hat and hangs them up.)

Ma (greets him): Sue's gittin' married.

Pa (shows little interest): Sure enough? Whut wuz the matter with the feller?

Ma: Nuthin', I reckon. He looked like he had good sense.

(Pa goes over and lights candle in holder.)

Ma (yells at him): Blow that candle out. Wanta set this place afire?

(Pa blows, but with lower lip extended over upper lip, he is unsuccessful.)

Pa: I can't blow it out. You try it.

(Ma tries, but since her upper lip extends over the lower lip, she, too, is unsuccessful.)

Ma: I can't do it, Pa.

(Sue and Zeke return.)

Ma: Come here, Sue, and blow out this candle.

(Sue tries, blowing out of the left side of her mouth. She fails.)

Sue (to her new husband): Zeke, blow out this candle.

(Zeke blows out of the right side of his mouth. The candle still burns.)

Zeke: Shucks! Missed it! I got an idee! Let's all blow together.

(The entire family gathers round and blows, and the candle is extinguished.

CURTAIN

Precious Priscilla—All italicized parts are read by someone and the characters pantomime their parts. The reader introduces all the characters and then begins the story, being careful to speak clearly and distinctly so the audience will have no trouble understanding.

CAST

Precious Priscilla, the pretty princess (flutters to the center of the stage, curtsies, bows, and exits)

Pious Paul, a peppy pal (dressed in gypsy costume, comes in taking long steps, tips his hat several times to the audience, and exits)

Petrified Pete, the Pawnee papa (comes on the stage stealthily and scowls at the crowd)

Prevaricatin' Pat, the Pawnee's partner (follows just a few steps behind Pete and imitates him exactly)

Peggy Peruny, the poisonous prattler (is indifferent to everybody)

Primitive Polly, the plucky pet of the plains (is snappy, comes in with hands on hips; may be a gypsy)

STORY

Precious Priscilla, the pretty princess, parts from the palace for the prosperous plains. (She walks across the stage backward, throwing kisses toward the wings, and runs into Pious Paul, who has been watching her with interest. She shows surprise. He suggests a walk, offers his arm, and they leave in the direction Priscilla was going.)

Primitive Polly peers 'pon her pal and Precious Priscilla. Her poor pulse palpitates painfully. (Polly enters, registers jealousy.)

Petrified Pete and Prevaricatin' Pat plot to pounce 'pon Precious Priscilla and plunder the plains. (Pete and Pat tiptoe stiffly to center stage, plot together, scan the horizon. They go to opposite corners of the stage, then come back to center.)

They park behind a pile of pebbles. (They take two or three steps and squat.)

Precious Priscilla plods the plains plucking posies. (She zigzags over the stage, very elaborately breaking off flowers, occasionally smelling the bunch. She even picks some off Pete's head, ignoring the fact that he is there.)

She sits on prickly pear. (You know the action.)

She perches 'pon peanut near pebbles. (She assumes sitting posture beside Pete and Pat.)

Pete and Pat pounce 'pon her. (They creep up on either side and grab her. Priscilla registers screaming. They gag her and swing her back and forth as though wrestling.)

They put her 'pon pony and part from plains. (The three step back, take high steps as though mounting, and gallop off, Pete pulling reins, Priscilla screaming, Pat slapping an imaginary horse. They may use broomsticks or just imagine they are on horses. Height contrast is wanted here.)

Primitive Polly peers 'pon them and promptly protects Priscilla by persuading Paul to pursue. (Enter Paul on horseback. He stops and acts dismounting, listens to Polly, motions her up behind. They gallop off.)

Pete and Pat progress. (They gallop across stage left to right, going in circles.)

Paul's prancing pony is pricked by pointed posies and grows punk. (Both hop heavily on one foot, dragging other.)

Pete procures paddlewagon and proceeds. (They paddle slowly.)

Paul and Polly procure another paddlewagon and resume pursuit. (Paul in front takes long dignified strokes, Polly behind takes short, wild dashes as they approach center stage.)

Paul's paddlewagon hits pesky protruding prong. (Polly goes over the side. Three short strokes, one long one, Polly climbs back in, then all is as calm as before.)

Peruny is perched 'pon pallet, perplexed at Pete's not producing plunder. (She comes in and squats at back center.)

Pete pitilessly pitches Precious Priscilla 'pon pallet. Produces poison and plans to poison her. (Have large bottle labeled poison with water inside. They try to make her drink the poison.)

Paul and Polly prevent poisoning by pitching pepper at Pawnee. (Much sneezing and Pawnee falls over dead.)

Primitive Polly, having played her part, plunges penknife into her penetrable part and pays the penalty. (While the lovers embrace, Polly in center stage takes knife and with great deliberation stabs herself. She first tries to make it go in her head, then stabs her heart and falls over backward. Paul goes to her side, feels her pulse, sees she is dead. Returns to Priscilla. They look regretfully at Polly. Paul takes off his hat, Priscilla wipes a tear.)

CURTAIN

From *The New Fun Encyclopedia,* Vol. 2, *Parties and Banquets,* pp. 58-61.

The "Ah" Skit—The only word spoken in the play is "Ah." This skit must be well done to be effective. Everything depends on the dramatic action and voice inflection.

CAST

Hero	*Thief*	*Father*
Heroine	*Cop*	*Mother*
	Maid	

Maid enters singing (to tune of "Auld Lang Syne") "Ah-ah-ah-ah-ah-ah-ah-ah-ah-ah-ah-ah-ah-ah." As she dusts, she hears the approach of the heroine and her lover. Gives a disgusted "Ah." Exits.

Hero and *Heroine* enter. Seat selves on sofa, sighing "Ah!" Look into each other's eyes and both give romantic "Ahs."

Hero draws a jewel case from his pocket, opens it, offers it to heroine.

Heroine gives a delighted "Ah!"

Hero rises to leave. Both express disappointment that it is time for him to go by their "Ahs."

Hero leaves, followed by a sighing "Ah" from *Heroine.*

Mother and *Father* enter.

Heroine excitedly shows them the jewel.

Mother gives a pleased "Ah" of admiration.

Father grunts a disinterested "Ah." Parents exit.

Heroine stands admiring jewel. Decides to put it away for the night. Places it in jewelry box. Exits. Lights are turned low.

Thief sneaks in. Discovers jewel. Gives a satisfied "Ah." Hears someone approach. Gives a stealthy and frightened "Ah." Attempts to hide behind screen.

Maid enters. Sees thief. Screams "Ah!"

Family rushes in. Variety of "Ahs."

Thief tries to escape but finds all exits blocked. Gasps frightened "Ahs."

Cop enters. Sees thief and emits a knowing "Ah!"

Thief gives a despairing "Ah!"

Cop nabs thief, with a satisfied "Ah."

Thief leaves with cop, exclaiming a disgusted "Ah."

Family sighs together an "Ah" of relief.

CURTAIN

The Saga of Little Nell—This mountain tragedy takes place in a poverty-stricken hut on Christmas Eve. Broken-down chairs, boxes, turned-over buckets and other seats will be needed for the family.

CAST

Mammy (clothed in ill-fitting dress, sunbonnet, apron)

Pappy (ragged overalls)

Little Nell, eldest daughter (ragged dress, wig of long yellow curls)

Handlebar Hank, the villain (large person with black mustache, dressed in black coat and hat, high boots)

Jack Dashaway, the hero (small person with high voice, wearing sissy outfit or riding pants and tight jacket)

Five or Six Other Children (in ordinary clothes)

SCENE I

(It is bitter cold and snow is on the ground. Family is seated in the one room.)

Mammy (holding loaf of bread): Well, Pappy, here it is Christmas Eve, and this is our last bit o' vittles.

Pappy: Yes, Mammy. (Goes to door and peers out with hand shielding eyes.) 'Taint a fit night out for man nor beast, but Handlebar Hank will be here shore to collect his mortgage money. (Paper snow is thrown in his face through the doorway. He sits down beside Mammy.)

Mammy (desolately): Yes, and we have not a cent fer to pay with. (There is a knock at the door.)

Second Child: Hark! I think I hear a rapping at the door. (Goes and opens door.)

Handlebar Hank (enters and swaggers about stage): I have come for my money or Little Nell.

Little Nell (waves arms, wrings hands—heavy acting—ends up on Pappy's shoulder): Oh-oh-oh-oh.

Third Child: 'Tis only a beast who would suggest such a plan.

Nell: Do not fear, little ones, Jack Dashaway will save us all.

Hank: Aha! Me proud beauty, I have you in my power at last. (Laughs sneering dirty laugh; flaunts mortgage paper at Nell.)

(Another knock at the door. *Third Child* opens door; hero enters.)

Jack Dashaway: I have heard all. Little Nell shall never become your wife. I will have the money here by midnight. (Goes to door, peers out, snow is thrown in his face.) 'Taint a fit night out for man nor beast. (Plunges into storm.)

Hank (surveys all sneeringly): I'll return at midnight. 'Taint a fit night out for man nor beast. (Opens door; paper snow is thrown in his face.)

SCENE II

(Family shifts position to denote lapse of time. There is a knock at the door, *Third Child* opens door; *Hank* enters.)

Hank: I've come for ye, me proud beauty. (Grasps Nell's arm roughly. Everyone wails—Nell demonstrates extreme agony.)

Second Child (in monotonous voice): Her bosom heaved.

(Door bursts open; hero Jack enters.)

Jack: For shame. Release her instantly. Here's your money. Give me that mortgage. (Seizes paper. Family shows elation.)

Hank: Curses! Foiled again.

Jack: Scram, you popeyed pole kitty. (Climbs on box and socks villain. Hank sits down on floor in groggy condition.)

Pappy: You've certainly done right by our little Nell.

Jack: Come, Nell, let's away on our wedding trip. (Nell registers joy, takes Jack's arm.)

Third Child: She drew herself up to her full height.

Nell (walks across stage with Jack and flaunts mortgage paper under Hank's nose): We've got a deep lake on our farm. Drop in sometime.

CURTAIN

Bluebeard—Here is a play with dialog in rhyme. On pages 56-58 is a similar skit with non-rhyming dialog.

CAST

Bluebeard (with a beard made of blue yarn or crepe paper)

Fatima *Sister Ann* *Selim*

ACT I

(*Fatima* is on stage. *Bluebeard* enters.)

Bluebeard: Wife, I have come to say,
I find that I am called away.
I've so much business to transact
'Twill be a week before I'm back.

Fatima: Oh, Bluebeard, dear, how sad you make me.
Is that the way you would forsake me?
I don't see why you cannot take me.

Bluebeard: Although I think so much of you,
I do not think that it would do;
I fear that you would get the flu;
Perhaps you'd want a new hat, too.

Fatima: I declare that I won't get the flu,
In business I'll be aiding you.

Bluebeard: Women in business should not roam,
I say that you must stay at home.

(Enter *Sister Ann*)

Bluebeard: Sister Ann, prevent this strife,
Come here and reason with my wife.
If you'll but listen to my commands,
I'll leave the whole house in your hands.

Ann: Why, Bluebeard, you're a perfect duck.
I say, Fatima, we're in luck.
Think of anything nicer if you can
Than a whole quiet place without a man.

Fatima: You wouldn't think so, I'm afraid
If you were doomed to be an old maid;
Eligible men are scarce enough,
So grab 'em early and treat 'em rough.

Ann: Sure, Bluebeard, Kid, we'd love to stay;
Suppose you slip those keys this way;
Have you something else to say?

Bluebeard: Yes, that I have—now listen here,
Perhaps you'll think this slightly queer,
But one room is forever hid;
To open it, I you forbid.
This key I give you, but don't unlock
Or you will get an awful shock.
And if you do, I will find out,

And so, my dear, you must mind out.
Now fare you well—don't weep for me
And mind you—*don't forget the key.*
(Exits.)

Ann: I'm so excited I could burst;
What part shall we explore the first?

Fatima: I don't know—now let me see;
I can't forget that awful key.
The thought of that room seems so funny;
I wonder if it's full of money.

Ann: There's nothing there, men have no sense;
Just like to keep us in suspense.

Fatima: I know—I'll think of it no more;
But I wish I knew what's behind that door.

Ann: Oh, lots of junk, perhaps, who knows?
Probably just his winter clothes;
I know when Papa goes away,
If he has any time to stay,
He locks his clothes with iron clamps,
For fear Ma'll give them all to tramps.

Fatima: But then they should be aired, you know,
For in old clothes germs do breed so.
If this came to a nurse's eyes,
I'm sure she'd say to sterilize.
Do you really think Bluebeard would mind?
Ann, you'll do nothing of the kind.
I mean to be an old-fashioned wife
And obey my husband all my life.

Ann: But do you think he would refuse,
When we've got such a good excuse?

Fatima: Ann, stop teasing. You've simply got to,
You know that Bluebeard said not to.

Ann: I'd rather be single
My whole life through
Than to be bossed around like you.

Fatima: I hope you will be an old maid.
I'll show you that I'm not afraid.
Give me the key and draw up near.
You listen, Ann, let's see what's here.
(Opens door and drops key.)
O heavens, horrors, look, oh, dear,
I think that I will die with fear.
Oh, help me now my patron saint!
Ann, lock the door before I faint.

Ann: Oh, Fatima, what do I see—
And, Fatima, where's the key?

Fatima: Don't speak to me, I think I'll die.
I dropped the key—Ann, oh, my!

Ann: Oh, Fatima, we're lost for good,
For see, the key is smeared with blood.

Fatima: Ann, this is more than I can bear;
He'll hang me up there by the hair,
And when I'm withered up and dried,
I hope that you'll be satisfied.

Ann: Fatima, be calm, don't take on so,
We'll wash it clean with soap, you know.

ACT II
(One week later)

(Enter *Fatima* and *Ann*)

Fatima: Oh, Ann, whatever shall we do?
The blood is here as good as new.
Although we've scrubbed, he'll surely see
Just how the blood got on the key.

Ann: Every cleaning thing, we've tried it;
We'll simply take the key and hide it.
Make him forget—say how you miss him,
Beguile him with your charms—and kiss
him.

Fatima: Oh, if Selim would only come before
He puts *my* head behind that door.

Ann: He got our letter by last night's mail.
He'll come, surely he'll not fail.
He can save us, he can do it,
But will Bluebeard beat him to it?

Fatima: Poor little neck, you feel so small,
Think of hanging on that wall.

Ann: They look funny hanging so
Like dried onions in a row;
Will it console you when you're dead
To know you'll have the prettiest head?

Fatima: Oh, Ann, I think I hear his step.

Ann: Rush to him now, don't lose your pep.

Fatima: I didn't think 'twould be so quick,
Here he comes—oh, I'm just sick.

(Enter *Bluebeard*)

Bluebeard: Well, well, my dear, I'm back, you see,
And home looks mighty good to me.
Come here and kiss your loving man;
My! How I've missed you! How're you, Ann?

Fatima: Oh, Bluebeard, oh, dear, I'm so glad!
The whole long week has been so sad.
I know you're tired. Oh, what a pity!
Now tell me all about the city.

Bluebeard: Well, Baghdad's going pretty slow.
No place like home, after all, you know.
How's everything? Been busy bees?
By the way, you haven't lost the keys?

Women: Oh, no.

Ann: Now sit down, Bluebeard, sit down, do.
Can't I get your pipe for you?

Fatima: And some nice hot coffee, I'll light the taper
So you can read the evening paper.

Bluebeard: You are most kind, too kind to me,
But first I'd like to have the keys.

Fatima: Why, certainly, I was just asking you,
Did you see anyone in town we knew?
(to *Ann*)
I can't stand the strain and worry.
Phone to Selim, make him hurry.

Bluebeard: I'll tell you later, if you please,
But first, my dear, I want the keys.

Fatima (handing him all but one):
Yes, here they are, now put them away;
Let's talk of something else today.

Bluebeard: Now, just a minute, not so fast.
Where is the key I gave you last?

Ann: Speak, Fatima, give him a hug.

Fatima: I think I dropped it under the rug.

Bluebeard: Speak, madam, speak, but don't evade me.
I fear that you have disobeyed me.
Stop hiding it—oh, yes, I see;
Whence came the gore upon the key?

Fatima: Oh, Bluebeard, don't; oh, please forgive,
I'll be so good! Oh, let me live.

Bluebeard: Don't plead with me, it's quite a bore,
And useless, too, with wives galore.
Since you've a fondness for that door,
You may hang in there forever more.
My knife needs sharpening. While upstairs,
I leave you here to say your prayers.

Ann: Oh, Fatima, I feel for you,
I really, truly, really do.
I always stood for a single life;
I'm glad that I'm not Bluebeard's wife.

Fatima: Let this be a lesson, Ann,
Never, never, trust a man.

If ever you approach the altar,
Think of my sad fate and falter.

Ann: Oh, if Selim would only come
And kill your Bluebeard, the old bum.

Fatima: Ann, look, I'm really too scared to pray;
Do you see anything coming this way?
(Climbs on a chair and peers into the distance.)

Ann: I think I do; oh, me; oh, my.
No, it's the milkman going by.

Fatima: Oh, look again, I think I'll die;
Do you see nothing riding by?

Ann: Oh, yes, I see something. But—oh, the dickens—
I believe it's just a flock of chickens.

Fatima: Ann, Ann, my time draws near,
Why isn't Selim hastening here?
Don't you see someone? Ann, you must!

Ann: I see a little cloud of dust.

(Enter *Bluebeard*)

Bluebeard: Well, madam, I hope you are prepared;
I'm sorry you could not be spared.
But I do feel, after deep reflection,
I need a new head in my collection.
It's my law, you know, and there's no repealing.
But I hope you'll bear me no hard feeling.

Fatima: Mercy, Bluebeard, mercy, pray!

Bluebeard: No, madam, no, just step this way.
You must be punished, faithless wife,
And feel the edge of this little knife.
(Starts to kill her.)

(*Selim* enters)

Selim: Down, villain, down, and bite the dust;
My dagger in thy heart I thrust.
(Kills him.)

Fatima: Oh, Selim, Selim, my noble lad,
You've spared the only life I had.

Ann: Oh, Selim, Selim, you're simply great,
Let's go somewhere to celebrate.

Selim: Quite right. Put on your hat and coat,
And we'll go get a chocolate float.

CURTAIN

What Fatima Saw—At the proper time, open door or draw aside curtain to disclose a gruesome sight: Heads of two or three of Bluebeard's former wives, seemingly detached from the bodies and hanging suspended by the hair.

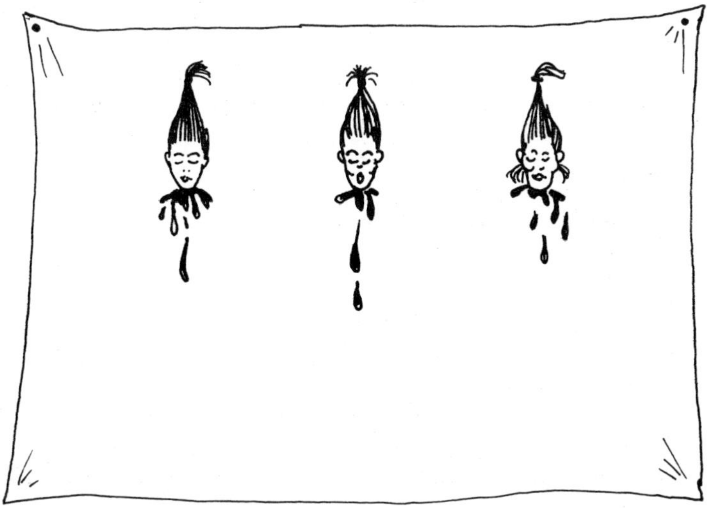

Girls put their heads through holes or slits in a sheet. Red ink blots appear below the necks. The faces are whitened for a ghastly appearance. The hair is tied to the sheet to make the heads appear to be hanging.

A Bluebeard Skit—If there is no door at the back of the stage, a curtain may be hung to hide from view the gruesome scene of the heads of Bluebeard's wives (see page 55).

CAST

Bluebeard	*May Knott,* the maid
Lessee, Mrs. Bluebeard	*Salvo,* the hero

SCENE I

(A room in the castle. *May Knott* is dusting the furniture and singing softly. *Lessee* is sitting in a rocking chair, reading.)

Lessee: You have a beautiful voice, May. Sing another for me.

May: Thanks, Mrs. Bluebeard. (Starts to sing again.)

Bluebeard (enters hurriedly; glares at maid): What's the matter with you? Sick? Sounds like static on a stormy night. (Turns to Mrs. B.) My dear, I'm going away on a business trip.

(*May* glares at him behind his back, makes a face.)

Lessee: I'm so sorry. I don't know what I'll do without you!

Bluebeard: Well, it has to be. And I'm leaving right away. Take this key and keep it for me till I return. It's the key to my secret room. See that no one enters that room. I'll kill anyone who opens that door! (Draws finger across throat in a significant gesture.) I must be gone. (Hurries to door, pauses, turns, and repeats the gesture.) Remember!! (Exits.)

Lessee (stands looking at key; muses): I've always wanted to see what is in that room.

May: Well, why not open the door?

Lessee: Oh, I'm afraid! Didn't you see the way he looked?

May: Sure, but his face looks terrible all the time. He'll never know! Come on! You're his wife. You have a right to know what's in that room!

Lessee: Well, just one peep.

(She unlocks door, throws it open, and both *May* and *Lessee* let out unearthly screams at the sight of the suspended heads. The door is immediately shut and locked. The key is dropped in the excitement and *Lessee* picks it up.)

Lessee: Oh, what'll I do? How can I explain this blood on the key? It won't rub off.

May: Tell him you cut your finger and got blood on it. And you'd better send for Salvo, your former sweetheart. He'll protect you against this human devil.

Lessee: Go and send word immediately to Salvo to hurry to my aid.

(*May* exits.)

SCENE II

(*Lessee* is pacing up and down, much disturbed.)

May (enters excitedly): Mr. Bluebeard is just driving up.

Lessee: Oh, what shall I do? What shall I do?

May: Just keep a stiff upper lip and stall him off until Salvo can get here.

Bluebeard (bursting in): Well, I'm back. Where's the key?

Lessee: I'm so glad you are back, dear. Did you have a good trip?

Bluebeard: Never mind the trip. Where's the key?

Lessee: Oh, the key? I'll get it for you directly.

Bluebeard: You'll do nothing of the sort. You'll get it now. Hand it over!

(Trembling, *Lessee* hands him the key.)

Bluebeard (looks at key, sees bloodstains, shouts): So you've disobeyed me, have you? Well, that's the end of you and of that loud-mouthed maid. Wait till I sharpen this knife. (Strides out, flourishing knife.)

(Sounds of grinding are heard. *Bluebeard* comes in occasionally to try knife on a piece of paper or a hair. Seems dissatisfied and goes back. All the while, *Lessee* is pacing, wringing her hands and pleading with May to look out the window to see if Salvo is coming. *May* is on a chair or ladder, peering into the distance.)

May: Ah, I see a cloud in the distance. It draws nearer, nearer, nearer. Oh, it's only Mr. ______, on his way to the golf course. (Pauses.) The moon is coming up over the hill. Oh, it's just Mr. ______'s bald head. (Pauses.) There's a strange speck on the horizon. Well, well, it's only Mr. ______'s mustache. (Pauses.) Oh, here he comes!! Here he comes!! He's riding like the wind. Courage, madam, Salvo is on his way. He's here! He's here! We are saved!

(*Bluebeard* enters, finally ready for the slaughter. But as he advances on the cowering women, *Salvo* dashes in, riding on a hobbyhorse. He draws a wooden sword and engages *Bluebeard* in combat. After a brief struggle, *Bluebeard* falls, mortally wounded. *Salvo* stands with one foot on Bluebeard and takes *Lessee* in his arms as she rushes to him.)

CURTAIN

Sofapillio—This skit will need a little scenery or a backdrop.

CAST

Rudebagio and *Spaghettio,* who are in love with Sofapillio
Sweep Uppio and *Sopolio,* maids of Sofapillio
Sofapillio, the heroine

(Cast enters.)

Spaghettio: I am Spaghettio, I love Sofapillio
But me she'll not havio, for she loves Rudebagio.

Rudebagio: I am Rudebagio, I love Sofapillio
And her will I marrio
To spite old Spaghettio.

Sweep Uppio (carries broom):
I am Sweep Uppio, the maid of Sofapillio;
The friend of Spaghettio, the foe of Rudebagio.

Sopolio (carries brush):
I am Sopolio, the maid of Sofapillio;
But I do not likio the way she does actio!

Sofapillio (surrounded by pillows):
I am Sofapillio. I don't know what to doio,
For two men do fightio to win my lovio.

(All characters exit except *Sopolio* and *Sweep Uppio*.)

SCENE I

Sopolio: Ho there, Sweep Uppio! What is the last reportio
of the love affairio of Sofapillio?

Sweep Uppio: Oh, it is worse than everio! It's enough to make one sweario,
That she keeps Spaghettio on the jumpio.

Sopolio: Oh, but she is a flirtio, but I know what I'll doio!
I'll go and help Spaghettio, for I hate Rudebagio,
Because he got my floor dirtio which I had just washed upio.

Sweep Uppio: Good for you, Sopolio, and I too will helpio
Every bit I canio to stop Rudebagio from winning Sofapillio.
For I just cannot standio the way she does actio.

Sopolio: Look, here comes Rudebagio. Let's get behind this bushio
And see what she doesio, then go and tell Spaghettio.

(Enter *Sofapillio* and *Rudebagio.*)

Sofapillio: Oh, it is you, Rudebagio? My heart it went thumpio
For fear it was Spaghettio. You know how I feario
To tell him that my lovio has gone from him to youio.

Rudebagio: My sweet Sofapillio!
Be it ever my endeavorio
To spare you any painio, but why not this avoidio
And with me elopio in my little Fordio
And to some preacher goio?
And we'll wedio this very nightio:
Then we'll take a tripio and to our home we'll goio
You as my wifio, my dear Sofapillio.

Sofapillio: My clever Rudebagio! Of all the rash thingsio
I ever heardio, this is the worstio!
But it does temptio my spirit of adventurio
And I will sure be readio to go with youio
This very same nightio when the moon comes upio.

Rudebagio: My brave Sofapillio! You have saved my lifeio,
For I was getting desperatio in my love for youio,
My dear Sofapillio. But I must awayio
And get the Fordio readio for our grand flightio,
Farewell, my sweet girlio!
(Kisses her hand, waves farewell, and exits.)

(*Sofapillio* goes into the house. The *maids* come out.)

Sweep Uppio: I am sure it was worthio the cramp in my legio
For sitting so stiffio behind that old bushio
To hear that grand plotio for the wild escapio.

Sopolio: And I, too, agreeio, that it was worthio—
But we must awayio to tell Spaghettio.

Sweep Uppio: Oh, there's no needio, for here he does comeio.
Say, do you knowio that old Rudebagio
And sweet Sofapillio are going to elopio
In the little Fordio, this very same nightio—
And they're going to wedio?

Spaghettio: This is not truio, for sweet Sofapillio
Is my betrothedio. How come you by this newsio?

Sopolio: We heard it just nowio behind this bushio,
And we saw as they plannedio that they would elopio.

Spaghettio: That blankety-blank Rudebagio! I'll get his goatio,
I'll make him payio! I'll spoil his schemio!
I'll make him deadio!
But thanks for the newsio. And now I must goio.

SCENE II

(*Spaghettio* and *maids* enter and look for a hiding place.)

Spaghettio: We'll hide hereio. Hark, here he comesio.

(They hide. *Rudebagio* enters.)

Rudebagio: Come, Sofapillio. The time is now hereio for us to elopio.

(*Sofapillio* enters, through a window, if possible.)

Sofapillio: Oh, Rudebagio, I cannot goio! I'm so scaredio!

Rudebagio: Hark, what is thatio? Ah, it's Spaghettio!

(*Spaghettio* and *maids* come from their hiding place.)

Spaghettio: I've got you, Rudebagio! I'll make you deadio.

We'll have a duelio with our stilettio.

(They fight, while *Sofapillio* runs around screaming. Finally both men fall dead.)

Sofapillio (on knees):

My heart is brokenio. I, too, shall dieio.
For one of my griefio cannot liveio.
Alas, I am deadio!
(Falls dead over Rudebagio.)

Sopolio (hits herself on the head with a spoon, falls):

Alas, I am deadio!

Sweep Uppio (falls dead):

Alas, I, too, am deadio!

CURTAIN

MAGIC

The secret of success in magic is, of course, to keep the spectators from discovering how a trick is done. The performer must practice each trick many times before a mirror in order to perfect the technique and must also learn how to evade the questions of friends. For just as soon as one friend learns how a trick is done, the news will spread until everyone knows the secret and it will cease to be fun for the crowd. Several rules might be set down:

Practice each trick in front of a mirror until it becomes natural and easy.

Never repeat a trick.

Never tell the audience what you intend to do.

Never tell how you did a trick.

Practice misdirection with your eyes. Your eyes should always look where you want the audience to look, regardless of what your hands are doing.

When something goes wrong, laugh and turn it into a joke, and the audience will laugh with you, not at you.

Work up some interesting patter to go with your tricks. This not only helps in misdirection but adds to the interest of the performance.

If you wish to keep up with current magic, it would be a good idea to subscribe to some good magic magazines.

Jumping Peg—A small peg which fits snugly into one hole in a small paddle is made to jump about from place to place, going from end to end. This trick depends upon the construction of the paddle. It has two holes going all the way through and two other holes, each of which goes only halfway through (see side view below). Holes 2 and 3 go all the way through. Holes 1 and 4 go only halfway through, and from opposite sides.

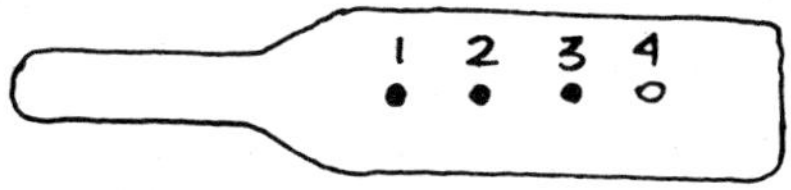

TOP VIEW

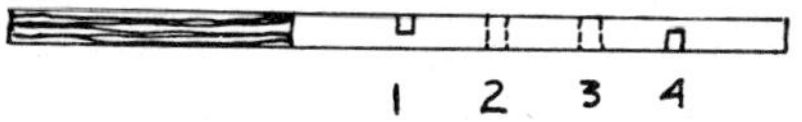

A special move apparently shows both sides of the paddle to the audience, but really shows one side. Suppose the little peg is placed in Hole 2. If the *A* side of the paddle is shown, the peg will appear to be in the hole nearest the handle, but if the *B* side is shown, it will appear to be in the center hole. Turn the paddle so that the *A* side is up and the peg appears to be in the hole nearest handle. Hold paddle between thumb and forefinger, in horizontal position pointing away from the body. Paddle is now swung up and back by twisting the wrist so as to reveal the *B* side, yet the peg is still apparently in the hole nearest handle. This is because the same side of paddle is shown. As it was swung up and back, the handle of the paddle was given a half turn between the fingers and thumb. The turning movement of the paddle is unnoticeable since the whole paddle is in motion. Actually, the same side of paddle is shown twice.

Then the paddle is given a shaking motion while held horizontally again, and it is turned over, making the peg appear to have jumped from one hole to another. Actually, the spectators are seeing the other side of paddle. The peg may be removed by hand and apparently placed back in the middle hole. But actually, the paddle has again been turned and the middle hole from side *A* would be No. 3, which, when turned over to show side *B*, would make the peg appear to have jumped to the extreme hole. Many simple routines can be worked out with this paddle after the one twist is mastered.

The paddle may be constructed in a very few minutes from a little wooden stick such as doctors use to depress tongues, or from an ice cream stick. The little peg may be a piece of match or toothpick, or any little piece of wood. Both ends of the peg should be alike, obviously.

The Invisible Hen—The performer shows a handkerchief and a hat, then folds the handkerchief and shakes it, repeating "cluck, cluck" or "kit-kit-ki-dat-cut," and an egg drops from the handkerchief into the hat. May be repeated many times and hat shown empty at close of trick.

Hat may be borrowed, but the handkerchief and egg are prepared beforehand. A wooden egg may be used, or the shell of an egg from which the contents have been blown out. This is fastened to the end of a black thread and the other end of the thread is attached to the center of one hem of the handkerchief, as shown in Figure 1, point *C*. The thread should be long enough to allow the egg to hang just about the center of the handkerchief.

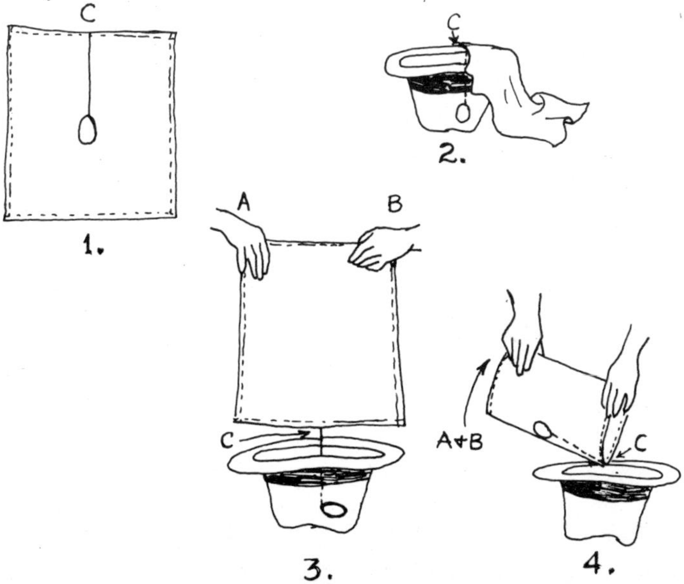

The borrowed hat is shown to be empty, and then the handkerchief, with egg concealed, is placed over the hat so that the egg is within the hat. The handkerchief is grasped at corners *A* and *B*, raised above the hat, and shown on both sides, the egg remaining in the hat during this showing. The handkerchief then is laid back on the hat and both hands are shown empty.

Next, the handkerchief is picked up with one hand at point *C,* being careful that the egg falls behind the handkerchief. The other hand may show the hat to be empty, if desired (first time only). Then put the hat down, double the handkerchief around the egg, hold it over the hat, and shake it as shown in Figure 4; the egg drops out into the hat as the magic words are said.

The same moves may be repeated (with exception of showing the hat empty) and several eggs apparently will be "laid" in the hat. The hat is then returned to its owner, who is surprised to find it empty. All the eggs have disappeared.

Removing Ring from String on Fingers—Tie the ends of a piece of string together, forming a loop. Thread a ring on the doubled string and slip the ends of the loop over the forefingers of a spectator, as seen in Figure 1. Without

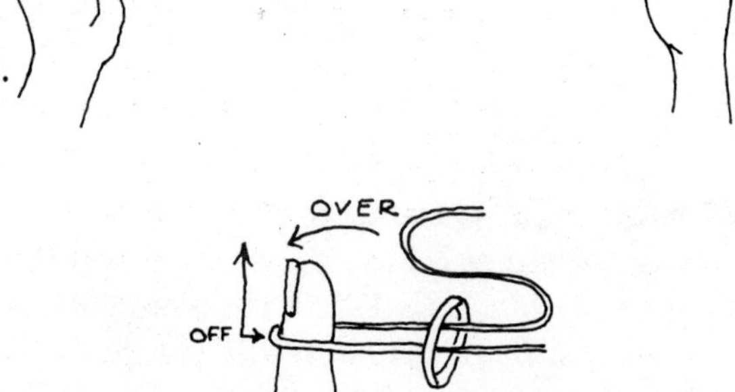

1.

2.

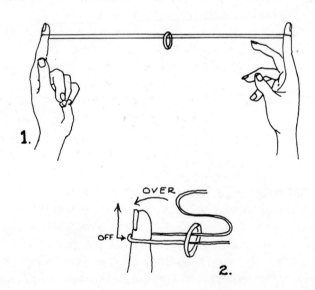

removing the string from the fingers, you can remove the ring from the string.

Slide the ring up close to one finger. Then loop one side of the string (as indicated in Figure 2) over the finger and remove the loop already there. The ring will immediately fall, yet the loop is still over the fingers.

Rope Release—Magician has someone tie both arms together at the wrists with a large handkerchief. A long piece of rope is now looped between the arms and around the handkerchief, and a spectator is asked to hold both ends of this rope and pull hard. The magician is able to get free of the rope without untying the handkerchief.

It is done this way: Work some slack in the long rope the spectator is holding. Pull the rope toward the fingers through the loose place in the handkerchief next to one wrist. This loop is then slipped over the hand and the magician may step backward free from the long rope.

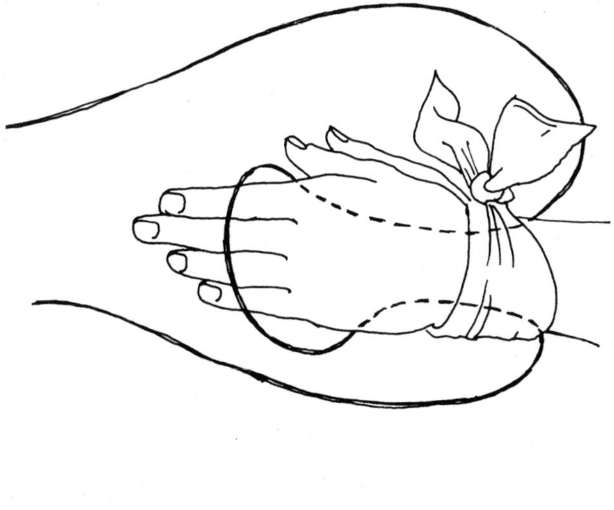

Restored String (Chewing Method)—A string two or three feet long is tied to make a circle or loop. It is then twisted to make a double loop and the audience is advised that if it were cut at any point, it would form two pieces of string, each having two ends. String is then opened out, and in the act of twisting it into a double loop again, an extra half twist is given so that it takes on the form shown.

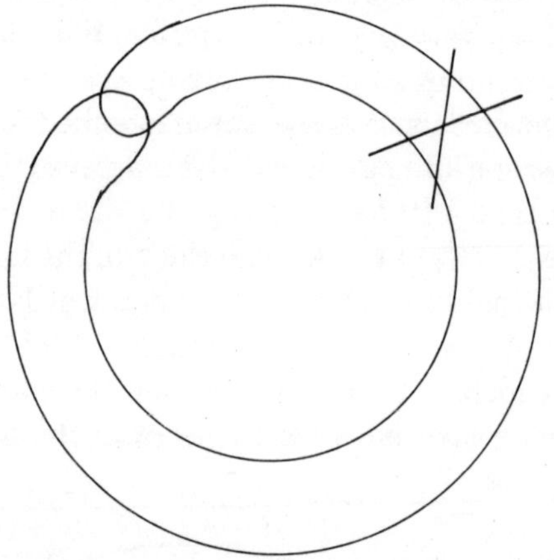

The performer covers up the twisted portion to prevent the spectators seeing this and asks someone to cut the string at the point marked X, the part held between the two hands. When the string has been cut, the two ends of the long piece are given to a spectator, and the two short ends are placed in the performer's mouth. These ends are always kept covered by the performer's hands.

The performer apparently causes the two ends to be chewed together, for when the string is pulled from the mouth, it is whole. What actually happens is that while the string is in the mouth, the performer removes the short piece of string and tucks it under the lip with the tongue, or disposes of it by hand before the string is shown "chewed together" again.

Restored String (Drinking Straw Method)—A drinking straw is shown with a string running through it. The performer bends the straw and cuts right through the center of it. Apparently the string is cut also, but when the sections of the straw are separated, the string is found to be restored.

The straw is prepared beforehand. With a razor blade, cut a slit about an inch or more long in the center of the straw, running lengthwise of the straw. When the straw is bent, the protuding ends of the string are pulled down, so that the center of the straw is cut above the hidden string. Thus the string is not cut with the straw.

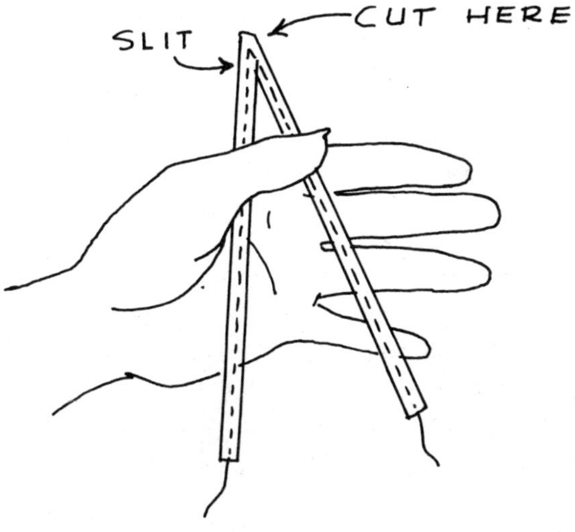

Coin and Matchbox—A matchbox is shown, empty inside. It is then closed and upon reopening, a coin is found within.

To prepare this trick, open the drawer of the matchbox half way and wedge a coin between the cover and the end of the drawer. In this position the box may be shown apparently empty, but when it is closed the coin drops into the drawer and appears there when the box is reopened.

Removing Ring from String—A ring is passed for examination, after which it is threaded on a string, the ends of which are held by spectators. While the ends are being held firmly, the ring is covered with a handkerchief, a special knot is tied, and one of the spectators is allowed to remove the ring.

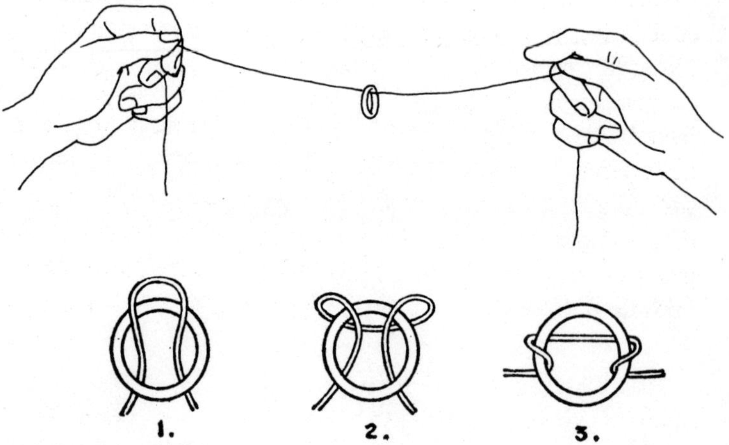

1. 2. 3.

Two rings, exactly alike, about one inch in diameter or slightly larger, are required to perform this trick. The string should be about three feet long. Conceal the duplicate ring in your left hand before the trick begins. Now have one of the spectators thread the ring onto the string, and give each end to a spectator. Throw the handkerchief over the ring. Under cover of the handkerchief, with your right hand grasp the ring that is actually on the string, covering it. Now take the duplicate ring concealed in your left hand and place it on the string as follows: Tell the spectators to give you a little slack so that you may tie a special knot. Pull the string through the duplicate ring as in Figure 1, and pass it over the ring as in Figure 2 until the string is tightened as in Figure 3.

Now ask the spectator on your left to remove the handkerchief. Tell the spectator on your right to take the ring in the left hand and the loop of string in the right and remove the ring. As the spectator does this, you, still concealing the original ring in your right hand, slide it along the string as if to take the string from the spectator on your right, while the spectator is using both hands to free the ring in the center. As soon as you slide the ring off the string, hand the end to a third spectator to hold while the ring is being removed. During this time you have ample opportunity to pocket the original ring. With a little practice this trick will bewilder the most intelligent audience. It is well worth the time it takes to learn it.

Two Thieves and Five Chickens—In this clever little mystery, seven little paper balls or pellets are used. The performer says that two of them represent thieves and the other five are chickens. Holding one pellet in each hand, the performer states that each hand is a barn in which a thief is hiding. The thieves steal the chickens, one by one: First one hand picks up a ball of paper, then the other, and so on, alternately, until all the paper balls have been gathered. Hearing a noise and thinking they are about to be caught, the thieves put back the chickens: The hands deposit five paper pellets on the table, one by one, alternately. As the noise subsides, the thieves again steal the chickens: Hands pick up the pellets alternately. But hearing the farmer coming to inspect his chicken house, the thieves escape to the other barn. To the surprise of everyone, when the hands are opened, the two thieves are found in one barn while the five chickens are in the other—one hand holds two paper balls while the other holds five.

This trick is accomplished by a very simple system. When the five pellets are picked up the first time, start with the right hand—pick them up as follows: right, left, right, left, right. In replacing five pellets on the table, start with the left hand—left, right, left, right, left. Most people will think you put back the same five you picked up. They will believe that each hand now contains one paper ball, whereas the right hand really holds two and the left hand none. Be careful to keep the left hand closed, as if it really contained the one they think is in it. In picking up the pellets the second time, begin with the right hand as before: right, left, right, left, right. Then when you open your hands, you will have five paper balls in the right hand and only two in the left.

The Magic Mothballs—This little mystery is a simple experiment in chemistry rather than a trick of magic. Fill a quart jar about three-fourths full of water. Stir into this about a spoonful of baking soda and an equal amount of citric acid crystals, which can be purchased at a drugstore. Then drop in six or eight round mothballs and watch the fun. It is more entertaining if the jar is placed in front of a lamp or a sunny window. The balls will go to the top of the water, turn over, and descend again continually for hours in a very orderly fashion. When the action slows down it may be speeded up again by the addition of a little more soda or citric acid.

Put Yourself Through a Card—Give each player a 3 × 5 card and a pair of scissors. The cards are to be cut so that a person could step through without tearing the card.

Fold the card lengthwise and make alternate parallel cuts (first on one side, then on the other), stopping ¼ inch from the opposite edge. Then cut through the folded edge, leaving the first loop on each end uncut. Open up and step through.

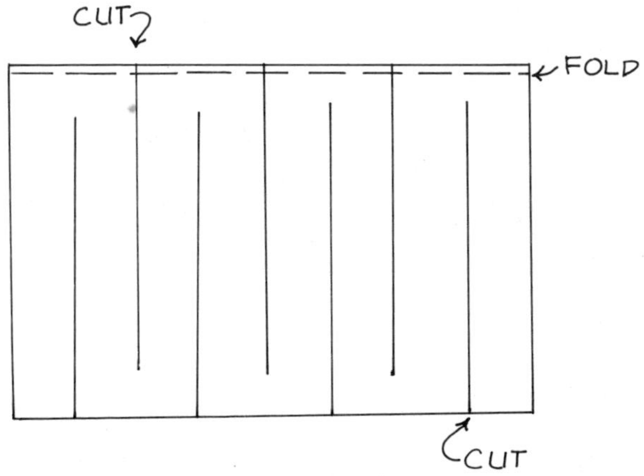

Hindu Mind Reader—People in the audience write questions on slips of paper and sign their names. These are collected by ushers who, unnoticed, pass the slips to a confederate at the rear of the room. The ushers then come back to the front and put fake slips on a large pan. A match is struck and the slips are burned. The mind reader looks on, but does not go near the slips. There is no possibility that the mind reader could read them. Then to everyone's amazement, the mind reader begins to call out questions and the names of the people who asked them. Each question is answered in some manner.

The mind reader wears a turban and robe. Under the turban there are earphones or an ear plug connected to a walkie-talkie or two-way radio. The confederate who received the slips from the ushers reads a few to the mind reader, who listens, pretending to be in deep thought. This trick should be rehearsed to be sure everything is working perfectly.

The French Drop—To make a small article vanish or to transfer it from one hand to the other, the French Drop is very useful and should be mastered by all magicians.

First, the coin is held between the thumb and forefinger of the left hand (see Figure 1). Next, the right hand moves

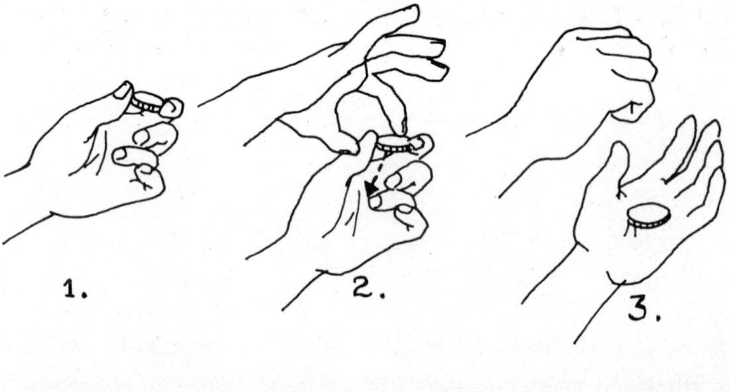

forward as if to take the coin, but just as the right fingers cover the coin, the left fingers release it and let it drop into the left palm, which should be held so as to hide the coin from the spectators. As the coin drops into the left hand, the right hand is closed, which causes the audience to believe the coin is in the right hand. The whole action must be blended into one quick movement. The left hand which contains the coin drops naturally to the side, and after the coin is shown vanished from the right hand, the left may produce it from some other position.

Make a Ruler Stick to the Hand—The laws of gravity are apparently defied as the performer makes a ruler stick to the palm of the hand. The figures below show how it looks and how it is done.

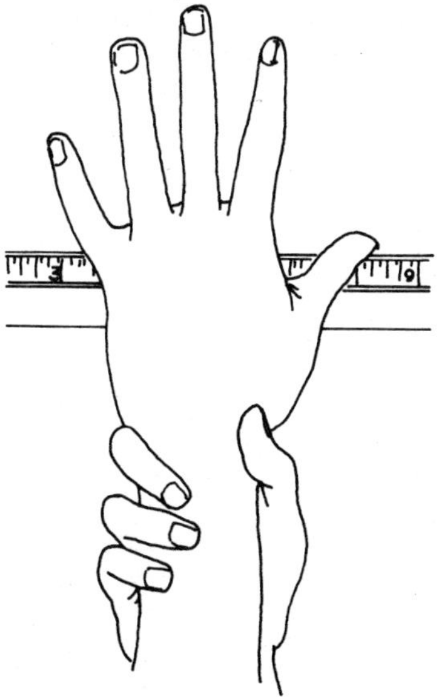

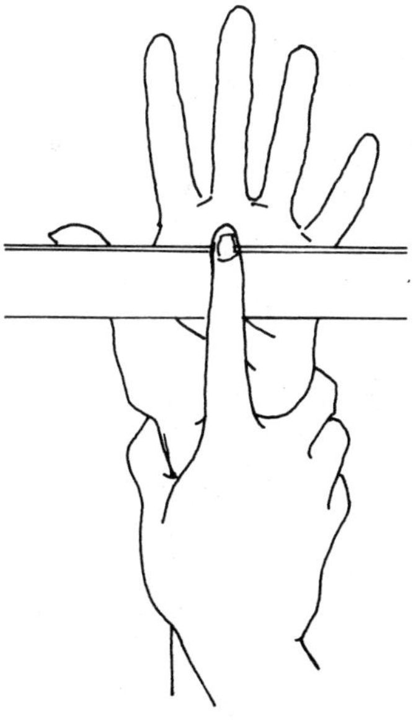

Place the ruler across the palm of the left hand, which is held in a horizontal position. Grasp the left wrist with your right hand and slowly raise the left arm, placing the index finger of the right hand over the ruler and keeping the back of the left hand toward the audience. The ruler will appear to be sticking to the left palm.

Which Hand Conceals the Coin?—Turn your back and ask someone to hold a coin in one hand. Tell this person to close both hands and hold them palms down. Then ask the person to raise the hand with the coin to the forehead, concentrate upon the coin for a moment, then lower the hand and say "Ready."

Turning around quickly, you will note that the hand holding the coin is whiter than the other, since while it was held to the forehead the blood circulation was retarded.

Traveling Coins—Four coins and two 3 × 5 cards or small envelopes are needed for this trick, one of the best small impromptu tricks ever performed. The coins should be placed on the four corners of an imaginary square, which should be on a bed or soft chair or cushion of some sort. The soft surface is needed in order to prevent noise when the coins are laid down, as well as to make them easier to pick up. The object of the trick is to cover the coins with the cards, yet cause them to travel mysteriously until all four come to Position 1.

Start by placing the coins in positions marked 1, 2, 3, and 4. Cover coin at 3 with card held in left hand, and coin at 4 with card held in right hand. Hold the cards over the coins—do not lay them down yet. State that the coins cannot be seen when covered with the cards because the cards are opaque. Then by crossing the hands, reverse the cards so that the right hand now covers No. 3 and the left hand covers No. 4. Announce that the coins cannot be seen when covered in this manner for the same reason.

1

2

3

4

Immediately, without stopping, continue the covering by placing right hand card over No. 2 and left hand card over No. 1. At this point the right forefinger goes under coin at No. 2 and picks it up under the card. Left hand brings the card over to cover Position No. 2, and just as it covers the place where coin No. 2 was, the card in right hand concealing coin No. 2 carries it over and places it down with coin No. 1.

Both cards are laid down at this point, and coin No. 3 is picked up and made to vanish with a throwing motion toward the card covering two coins now at No. 1. (The French Drop, described elsewhere, would be a good way to make the coin vanish, leaving it in the left hand.) When card now at No. 1 is picked up, it has two coins under it. One has apparently appeared there magically. In placing card back down, it is switched to left hand, which holds vanished coin, and the coin is placed down with the other two, under cover of the card in left hand. The coin now at No. 4 likewise vanishes and is apparently found under card at No. 1 with the other two. When card is replaced again it takes the last coin and adds it to the other three, under cover of replacing the card.

The spectators think a coin is still under card at position No. 2, so you apparently take a magic hair, push it down through the card, get the coin invisibly, and take it over and put it through the card at No. 1. Immediately all will want to see the result of this, so they watch eagerly as you pick up the card at No. 1, revealing all four coins, and the card at No. 2, revealing none.

All movements in this trick should be memorized so they can be done without a moment's hesitation. It is a clever trick and will be well worth the time it takes to master it.

Multiplying Currency—In preparation for this mystifying trick, fold a few dollar bills up into a neat wad and place it between the folds of your sleeve in the crook of your elbow. Having shown your hands empty, borrow a dollar bill as a starter, and as you show it, remark that there is nothing up your sleeves. To prove this, pull up your sleeves. When pulling up the sleeve that conceals the money, pick up the wad of bills. The audience will not see you do this, as they will be watching your sleeves, which you should do also. Pretend to roll the borrowed bill up into a little ball, of course adding the wad, and presently start taking many bills out of your hand, to the surprise of the spectators.

Right-side-up Matchbox—A box of safety matches, when flipped into the air, always lands right side up on the table.

A half-dollar was placed between the bottom of the container and the outside shell of the box. This gives just the right weight to cause the box to land right side up. The coin, of course, is secretly removed by the magician before someone else is challenged to try the trick.

Vanishing Coin (with Confederate)—Several persons are allowed to feel a coin that has been placed in a handkerchief, in order to prove it is really there. Finally the handkerchief is shaken out and the coin is gone.

The secret lies in the fact that you have a confederate in the audience who is the last to feel the coin and removes it from the handkerchief.

Smelling Out the Coin—Lay a row of pennies out on the table. Ask someone to take one of the pennies while you step out of the room, hold it tightly overhead, and concentrate on its position in the row. After a brief moment the person is to put it back in place. When you return to the room, you smell the coins and can tell the one that has been touched.

As you pretend to smell the coins, you actually allow your nose to touch the coins as you go from one to the next. Since copper is a good conductor of heat, and the nose is very sensitive to heat changes, it will be very easy to find the warmest coin in the group, and after a few sniffs, you can announce which coin was held.

Suspending a Coin on the Wall—Prepare a coin by cutting a small nick in one edge. A quarter is a good coin to use. The little sharp edge may be pressed into the wood of a wall and the coin will remain suspended.

Heads or Tails—While various members of the group spin a coin on the table, the performer, on the other side of room with back turned, announces each time whether the coin falls heads or tails.

The coin has a small nick in one side near the edge. When it falls with the nicked side down, it will have a flat sound and will stop spinning almost immediately. When the nicked side is up, the coin will spin much longer and have a gradually diminishing ring. A few tries will make it very easy, since you will know what to listen for.

Vanishing Coin (with Soap)—A coin placed in performer's hand vanishes when hand is closed and reopened.

Place a small piece of soft soap on the fingernail of your second or third finger. Put the coin in your palm where this finger will contact it when your hand is closed. Show the coin there, then close your fist, letting the coin adhere to the soap. Open your hand and the coin has disappeared. It is stuck to the back of your hand and cannot be seen from the front. Be careful not to turn your hand over.

The Broken Match Restored—To prepare, insert a match into the hem of a large handkerchief. Have another match marked and place it in the center of the handkerchief. It is then folded into the handkerchief and apparently broken, yet when the handkerchief is shaken out, the match falls to the floor completely restored.

The secret, of course, is that the match in the hem is folded into the center and broken by the spectator, while the performer holds the marked match safely in the folds of the handkerchief and shakes it to the floor. Dispose of the handkerchief while the match is being examined.

The Ring That Climbs—A borrowed ring is dropped over a pencil which the performer holds vertically. On command, the ring rises or falls or jumps completely off the pencil.

The pencil has a fine black thread fastened to its top and wound round a button on your clothes. As you move your hand away, the thread tightens and causes the ring to ascend. The thread will be invisible at short distance especially if you wear dark clothing.

If the pencil is reversed and the end to which the thread is fastened is held downward, then by moving the hand back and forth, the pencil itself may be caused to rise and fall. In this case no ring would be used. The thread may be fastened to the end of the pencil simply by cutting a slit in the end and passing the thread tightly through it.

Magic Writing—An apparently blank piece of paper may be shown the audience, passed for examination, or even signed by one of the spectators. Yet upon holding it over a lighted candle or other heat source, a message mysteriously appears on it.

Before the performance, make "ink" out of lemon juice and write any message desired on the paper. The writing will be invisible until the heat of the candle is applied to it. The heat reveals the secret message.

Many a Miss (Fifteen Matches)—Place fifteen matches in a row. One player begins at one end and another at the other. Each may pick up one, two, or three matches at a turn. The object of the game is to force the opponent to take the last match. It sounds simple but there will be many a miss for those who do not know the trick.

To win, of course, you must pick up the fourteenth match. In order to be sure of this, you must also get the tenth match. It will be well for you to try also to get the second and the sixth. If you count them as they are picked up, you will have no trouble winning, no matter who goes first.

Bottoms-up Mystery—Three glasses are placed in a row—the two end ones upside down and the middle one right side up. The object of the trick is to pick up the glasses two at a time and, in three turns, finish with all three glasses right side up.

When the moves are made rapidly it will be very hard for anyone to follow. Numbering the glasses 1, 2, 3, in order from left to right, first turn over 2 and 3, next 1 and 3, and last, 2 and 3. You will note that No. 3 is turned each time.

An interesting follow-up is simply to turn over the center glass now so that it is upside down (while the other two are right side up) and ask someone to duplicate your feat. Not one in a hundred will realize that the glasses are reversed from the way you started, and even though they catch your moves, they will end up with the glasses all bottoms up instead of upright.

Unbuttonhole—A string that has been tied into a circle is threaded through a buttonhole of performer's clothing, so that a loop of the string is on either side of the buttonhole. The ends of these loops are now caught over the thumbs (which are pointing forward and upward). The object of the illusion is to get the string out of the buttonhole and still have it on the thumbs.

With the little finger of each hand, reach over and catch the opposite top string from the under side; holding these strings on little fingers, bring hands back to first position. With the strings hooked around each thumb and little finger in this manner, let go of string with the right little finger and the left thumb. Pull on the string quickly, and as the string comes clear, the left thumb is slipped into the loop on left little finger as the left little finger is removed. This last move is made so quickly that the spectators do not notice the change of fingers.

This same method may be used to pull the string through the neck, although a longer loop of string will probably be required.

Contact Telegraphy—This little magic stunt is performed by two people, the magician and an assistant. The assistant goes out of the room while the audience gives the magician a number to be transmitted. The assistant returns and places hands on each side of the magician's head so that the fingers are on the magician's temples. A few seconds later, the assistant announces the number.

It appears to be mind reading, although there is really no mind reading to it. The magician signals by slightly tightening the lower jaw, causing the temples to press slightly against the assistant's fingers. Suppose the number were 273. The magician would press the jaw twice, signifying two; after a brief pause, seven presses; after another pause, three presses. Zero is transmitted with ten presses.

The Rising Ruler—A foot ruler is held in the magician's hand. Upon command it rises.

A rubber band is slipped around the first two fingers of the right hand, and the ruler is pushed down into the loop of the band inside the hand. Pressure of the fist holds the ruler in place. When the pressure is released, it will rise slowly, or even jump from the hand. Care should be taken not to push the ruler so far down that the audience sees the rubber band.

Grandmother's Necklace or **The Indian Beads**—This is a favorite trick of the Hindu magicians. Three beads are strung on two cords. The ends of the cords are held by spectators, yet the magician removes the beads without damaging them or the cords.

This trick can be easily understood by referring to the figure on the next page. Examine this illustration closely for the manner of threading the beads on the strings.

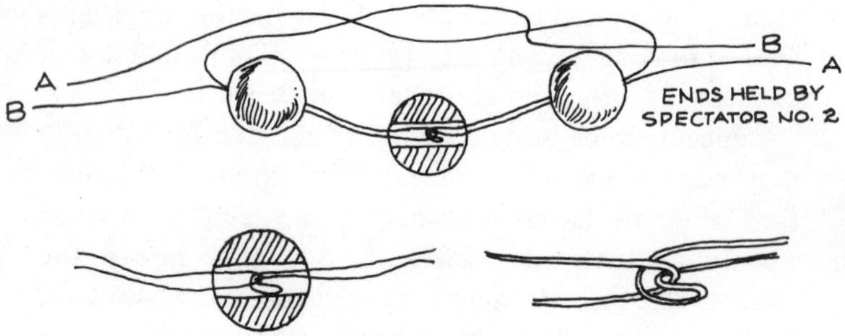

Show the three beads threaded on the strings and ask spectators to take the strings at each end and to hand you one string for each end, in order to tie the beads on securely. (This is really done to reverse the ends of strings.) Then, under cover of hand or handkerchief, pull the strings out of the beads and they will come off and all may be examined.

Mysterious Paper Bands—Take three strips of paper about fifteen inches long and one inch wide. Glue or tape the ends of first strip together to form a ring as in Figure 1. Make one complete twist with one end of the second strip as in Figure 2 and glue or tape the ends together to form a ring. Then make two complete twists with one end of the third strip as in Figure 3 and glue or tape the ends together to form a ring.

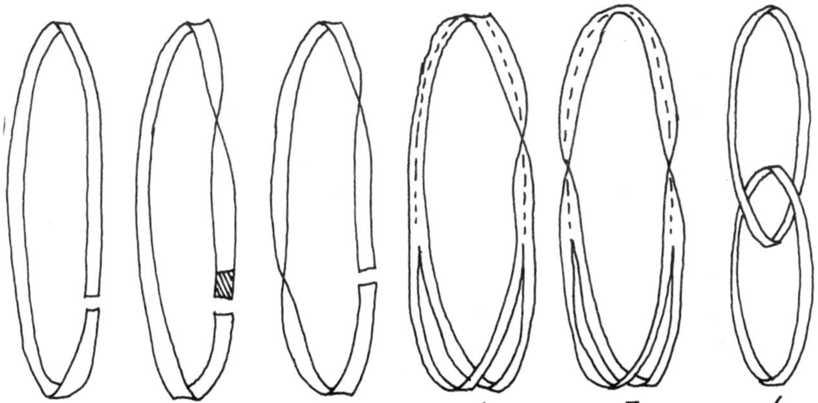

Punch a small hole in the center of each of these three strips and cut them lengthwise with scissors. The first one will form two rings of half width, disconnected (not shown). The second will be cut as in Figure 4 and will form a paper ring twice as large as the original. The third one will be cut as in Figure 5 and will form two rings, linked together in a chain as seen in Figure 6. Larger rings may be made according to same plans and used for decorations or other purposes.

The Pencil in the Buttonhole—A small wooden stick or pencil with a loop of cord through its eraser end is looped into a buttonhole. The loop of string is so much shorter than the pencil that it seems impossible to loop it, yet the magician does it very easily.

First put the entire loop over the cloth around the buttonhole and pull the material through the loop. Then put the point of the pencil through the buttonhole, pull the pencil through, and slip the loop of string off the cloth. To remove the pencil, simply reverse the moves. You should learn to do this so quickly that no one will notice the method. Then see if anyone can take the pencil off after you have put it on.

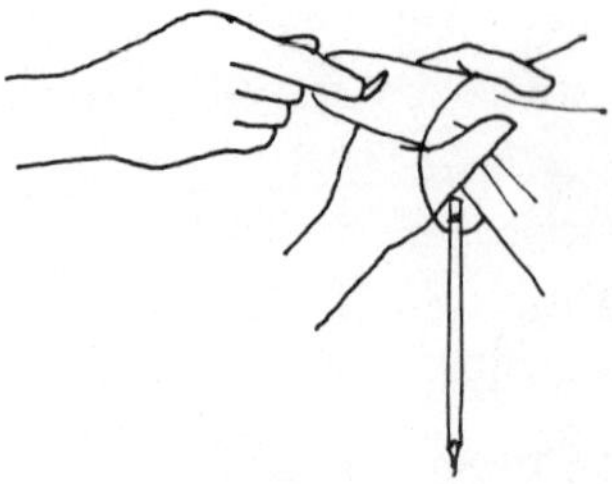

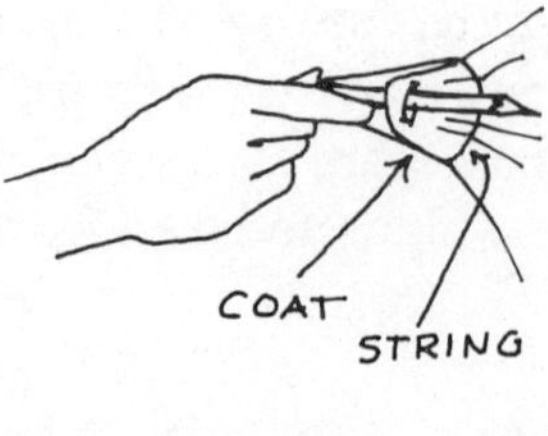

PUPPETRY

It's fun to make puppets. It's fun to play or perform with puppets. But it also takes patience and plenty of practice.

If a group desires to organize a puppet team to perform for the church or for clubs or other groups, the director must know all aspects of budget requirements, have the know-how to make, repair, or purchase puppets, and be aware of the intricacies involved in procuring scenery and props and arranging for lighting, costumes, scripts, and sound. The length of rehearsals and performances must be considered, and rehearsal schedules must be made out and distributed to team members.

Each member of the team should have an assignment unless there are enough volunteers to help construct equipment (puppet stage) and handle lights and sound equipment. Each member must learn how to manipulate puppets and how to develop a puppet into a personality. It is also essential to lip sync for puppets with movable mouths.

Resources for becoming an effective puppeteer are listed in the Bibliography. Here are some suggestions for making puppets.

Paper-Plate Puppet—

Materials: Paper plate, felt-tip marker, various colors of construction paper, piece of red cloth, glue, scissors.

Instructions: Fold the paper plate in half. Make eyes from construction paper and tongue from red material. Glue in place and decorate with felt-tip marker (see illustration, next page).

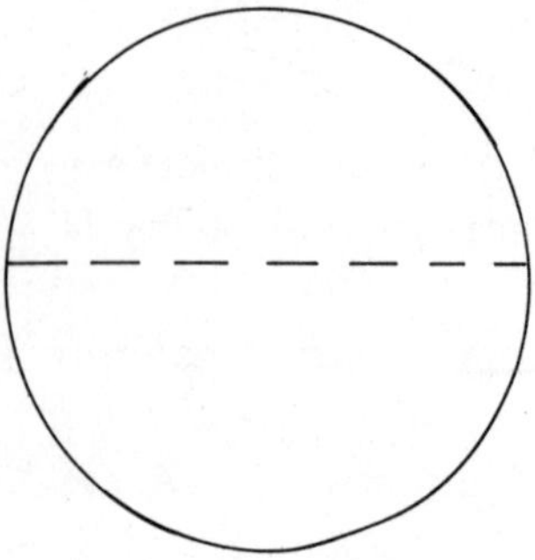

1.

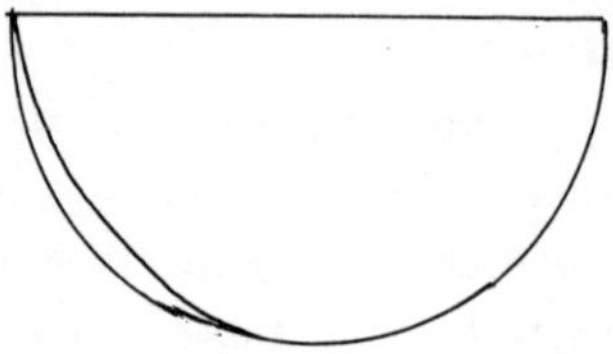

2.

3.

Construction-Paper Puppet—

Materials: Construction paper, glue, scissors, felt-tip markers, kite string, paper-towel tube, yarn or cut paper.

Instructions: Follow illustrations until puppet resembles Figure 8. Paper then may be doubled over as in Figure 9. Punch small holes in top and bottom and run string through, making a knot on top (Figure 10). Place paper-towel tube on bottom portion of string (Figure 11). Mouth may be opened and closed by manipulating the tube while hand is out of sight. Decorate with felt-tip markers and imagination. Hair may be made with yarn or cut paper.

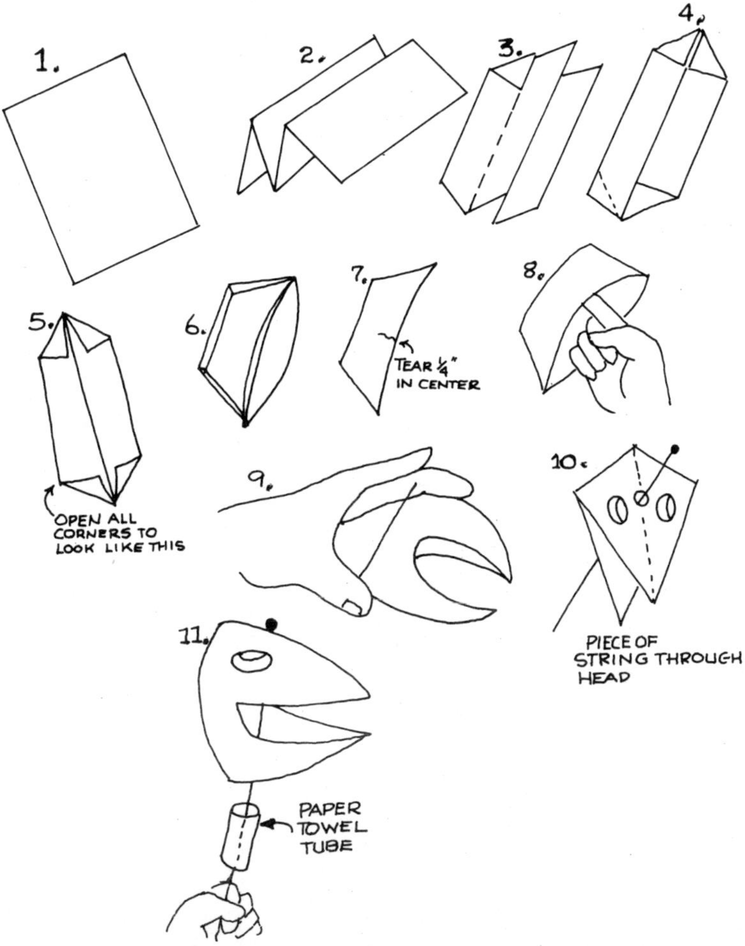

Adapted from Bob Sessoms, "Additional Day Camp Crafts: Indian Theme," *Church Recreation Magazine* (April/May/June 1974), pp. 28-29.

Cereal-Box Puppet—

Materials: One medium-sized cereal box *or* two miniature cereal boxes, construction paper, masking tape, stapler, felt-tip markers.

Instructions for Medium Cereal-Box Puppet (Figure 1): Cut cereal box almost in half. Staple or tape for strength. Decorate with construction paper and felt-tip markers. Insert hand into open box to manipulate.

Instructions for Miniature Cereal-Box Puppet (Figure 2): Place one box on top of the other. Tape or staple together at one end. Decorate with construction paper and felt-tip markers.

1.

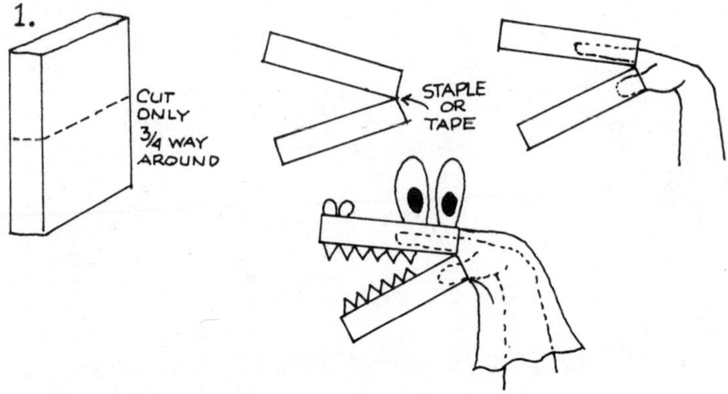

2.

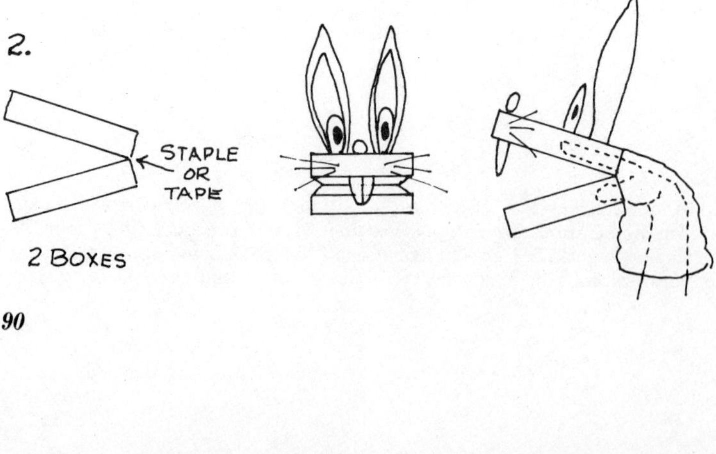

Paper-Sack Puppet—

Materials: A #1 paper sack (lunch bag), scissors, glue, construction paper, felt-tip markers, yarn or cut paper.

Instructions: Design a face on the sack, use yarn or cut paper for hair, and cut out construction paper for clothes, if desired (see illustrations). Insert hand to manipulate. One bottom fold forms the puppet's mouth.

Sock Puppet—

Materials: Heavy white cotton sock, buttons, thread and needles, glue, buckram, piece of red cloth, yarn, material for costume.

Instructions: Cut the red cloth into a 3 × 6½-inch oval shape. Cut the buckram (Figure 1) slightly smaller than the red piece and place it between the sock and the red piece on the sole of the sock near the toe. Stitch all around (see Figure 2). This is the puppet's mouth. Tuck in the heel and stitch down, making the sole and leg of the sock one surface. For eyes, sew on buttons; for hair, glue on yarn. For a costume, cut out a piece of cloth with a 14-inch radius. Cut a hole in the center and stitch to puppet.

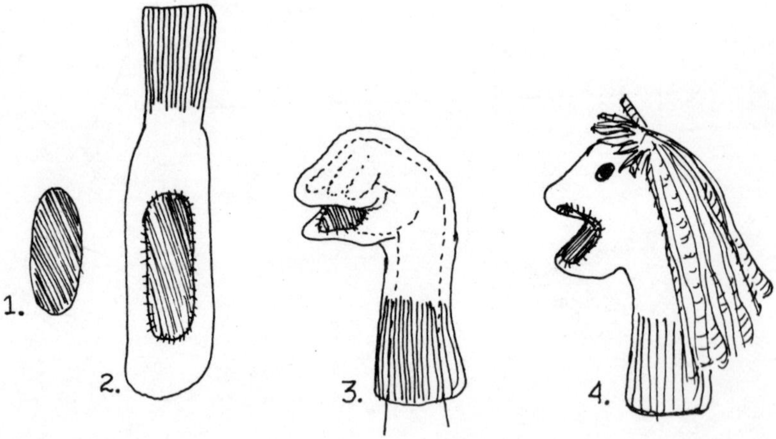

Styrofoam Puppet—

Materials: Styrofoam ball (3, 4, or 5-inch size), glue, pencil, buttons, latex wall paint, brushes, yarn or an old wig, material for costume.

Instructions: With a pencil, mark off features on the head (nose area, eye sockets, mouth, cheeks). Shape the head by pressing and squeezing the features into shape (Figure 1). When the features have been designed as desired, make a hole about the size of your index finger in the bottom of the styrofoam ball where the neck should be (Figure 2).

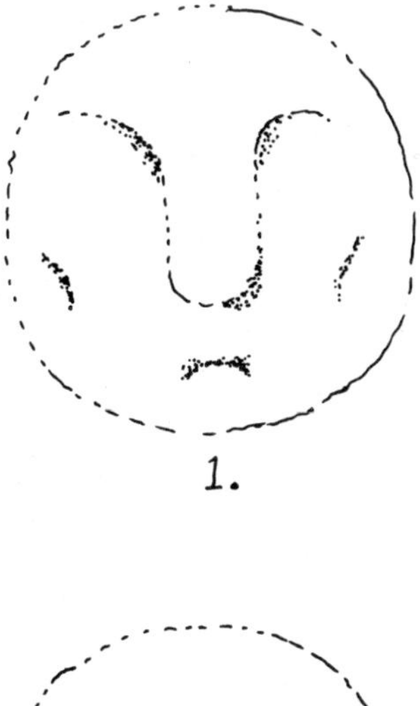

1.

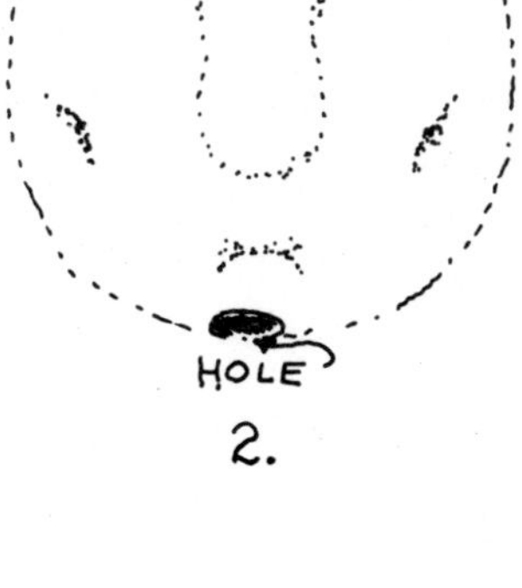

2.

Obtain flesh color paint by experimenting, or let the dealer do it for you. Use three coats on the head. Then paint the features. Colorful buttons may be glued into the sockets for eyes. For hair, eyebrows, and mustache, use yarn or an old wig or fur (Figure 3).

Cut out the costume. Place glue in the neck hole. With your index finger, push the costume into the hole as far as you can. Slowly remove your finger. Let dry for a couple of days (Figure 4).

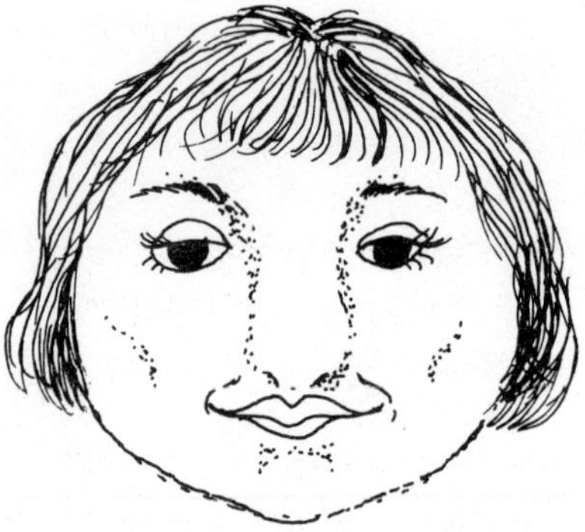

3.

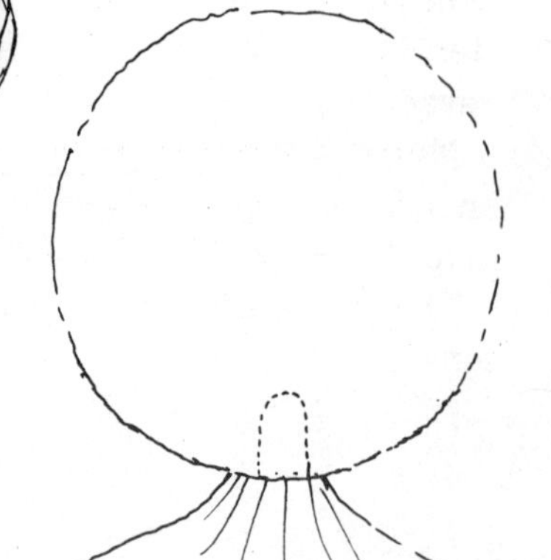

4.

Adapted from *Using Puppetry in the Church* by Everett Robertson.

2

FUN WITH MUSIC

Volumes have been written about music. It has been said that music is a compulsion, a force that shapes human destiny, a language of the spirit, an international language, a way to "soothe the savage breast." Music is eternal—a pleasing form of human expression that will never die.

Music is a source of pleasure, whether one sings, plays an instrument, or merely listens. As a form of recreation, it helps to create a much richer life-style for the individual.

This volume offers a few musical games, some action songs, and several old favorites, rounds, and spirituals.

MUSICAL ACTIVITIES

Songs and Musical Games—This is a good way to create a relaxed feeling in a group. It also helps control a crowd by bringing the people together.

Before one leads a fun sing-along or a musical game, certain guidelines should be kept in mind.

1. Know the directions for the game, the words to the song, and any movements that may accompany them.
2. Give clear instructions to the group.

3. Demonstrate! Sing the song with the group and demonstrate the actions.
4. If a game or song is not going well, try another.
5. Have an accompanist or play a tape so the people can hear the tune.
6. Know the basics of leading a song:
   —sing it through
   —have the group sing with you
   —go over the parts that seemed unclear or confusing
   —use the common methods for conducting. The arrows in the following illustrations show how the hand should move.

Two-four (2/4) Time

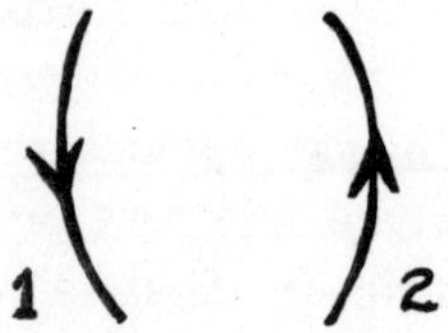

Three-four (3/4) Time

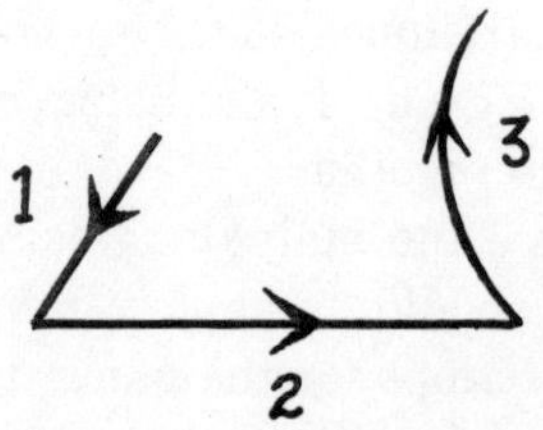

Four-four (4/4) Time

7. Practice!

Here are a few more musical activities for your consideration. Not every individual will want to take part in all these, but a selected group would enjoy any one of them.

Choirs—In organizing a choir, some decisions need to be made:

1. Who will direct the choir?
2. What age group(s) will participate?
3. What is the purpose of the choir?
4. Where will the choir perform? Where will it rehearse?
5. Who will be the accompanist?
6. What type music will be sung?
7. Will there be elected officers?
8. Will the choir tour?

From the choir, several groups can be developed:

An A Cappella Choir
Madrigal Singers
Quartets, Trios, Ensembles
Soloists

Choirs demand loyalty and commitment, and there should be some degree of musical ability on the part of the participants. Choirs should function for the enjoyment of both the participants and the listeners. Some are organized for the sheer pleasure of singing.

Orchestra or **Band**—People who played musical instruments in high school or college often stop playing after graduation. The formation of an orchestra or band would enable these musicians to enjoy their skills during adulthood. Again, the key is a top-notch organization with qualified leadership—from director to stage hand. From this attempt, other instrumental groups may emerge:

String ensemble
Brass ensemble
Wind ensemble
Jazz band

Musicians enjoy participating; others enjoy listening.

Music Classes—If there is interest on the part of the members of an organization, classes may be formed to help those interested in learning to sing or play musical instruments.

Kazoo Band—There are a variety of these types of bands. One might purchase kazoos in the shapes of miniature trumpets, trombones, clarinets, saxophones. Cymbals, rhythm sticks, tambourines, and triangles can add to the effect. Even an "instant" band can perform.

Handbell Choirs—These choirs are found primarily in church music programs. Handbells are expensive and must be properly cared for. Qualified leadership is especially needed for this unique musical activity.

MUSICAL GAMES

Here are several games that include music. The directions should be learned before a game is attempted. Demonstrate, and be clear in your instructions.

Nursery Rhyme Game

To the tune of "The Noble Duke of York" (above), sing the letters of the alphabet. When everyone has this down pat, sing a nursery rhyme to the tune. Try this:

Mary had a little lamb,
Its fleece was white as snow;
And everywhere that Mary went,
The lamb was sure to go.

Now divide into smaller groups. Give them a moment to think up nursery rhymes. Have someone write down the names of the rhymes as they are sung. If a group repeats a rhyme already sung by another group, or if it cannot think of a nursery rhyme in time, it forfeits. Call on the groups at random.

The Peanut Song
(Tune: "Farmer in the Dell")

1. (Name of that singer) has some peanuts,
   ______ has some peanuts,
   ______ has some peanuts,
   And he's (she's) going to give them to you.
2. ______ has some candy, etc.,
   And he's (she's) going to give it to you.
3. ______ has confetti, etc.,
   And he's (she's) going to give it to you.
4. ______ has some flowers, etc.,
   And he's (she's) going to give them to you.
5. ______ has some chewing gum, etc.,
   And he's (she's) going to give it to you.
6. ______ has some rotten eggs, etc.,
   And he's (she's) going to give them to you.

Singers line up on platform and sing the song indicated. As they come to the line "And he's (she's) going to give them to you," the singer whose name has been mentioned tosses the peanuts, candy, confetti, and so on, to the crowd. The eggs are last. Sometime just before the "egg" singer's turn, the singer should "accidentally" drop one of the eggs. It falls to the floor (on a space covered with paper) and great is the fall thereof, for "all the King's horses, and all the King's men" can't put it together again. This egg was a real egg. The others are eggshells, the contents having been blown out. If desired, they may contain a little water or, better, confetti. There is some grunting, screaming, and ducking as the singer lets fly the handful of eggs at the crowd—one at a time, in rapid succession. Or the eggs may be distributed to the other singers and they all throw at once.

Promenade Concert—The players seat themselves in a circle, each adopting a musical instrument on which to perform. For instance, one chooses the violin and draws the right hand backward and forward with a vigorous action, as though drawing a bow across the instrument. Another takes the cornet and puffs out the cheeks to the utmost extent. Another beats an imaginary drum, while another, strumming with hands upon knees or table (real or imaginary), chooses piano. The banjo, comb and paper, triangle, cymbal, tambourine, hand organ, may all be represented.

Every player must imitate the action and, as closely as possible, the sound peculiar to the adopted instrument. The greatest enthusiasm must be thrown into the performance. All may be required to play the same tune or different tunes.

Gravity is indispensable (because next to impossible) and the slightest violation costs a forfeit.

The conductor sits cross-legged on a chair in the center of the circle, facing the back of another chair on which to beat time. When the music (?) is at its height and the greatest confusion prevails, the leader suddenly singles out one of the performers and asks why that person is at fault. The person thus unexpectedly pounced upon must immediately give some excuse, which must be in keeping with the nature of the instrument. For instance, the fiddler replies that the bridge was broken and the river couldn't be crossed; the pianist, that one of the keys of the instrument was left at home. Any delay or repetition of an excuse costs a forfeit.

Human Pipe Organ—Choose about twelve participants from the group, preferably those who have some musical ability. With a pitch pipe or piano, carefully tune up each person as a different note for the pipe organ. Then each person holds out the right hand, and the leader creates a tune by touching the hands.

The Band—Purchase a number of kazoos that resemble trumpets, trombones, and so on. Hand these out, select a tune, and have the band perform.

Ghoulish Quartet—On a sheet or large piece of cardboard, draw four ghoulish figures. Participants put their heads through holes or slits in the sheets. The quartet can put on white makeup to add to the effect as they sing ghost-type songs.

Name That Tune—Divide into two groups. The first three notes of a tune are played on a piano or some other instrument. Team One has the first opportunity to name the tune. If Team One can guess the song, 5 points are scored; if not, Team Two has a chance. If neither team is successful, a note is added each time until one of the teams guesses the tune. One point can be removed each time a note is added. The longer it takes to name a tune, the fewer points are scored. The team with most points wins.

Whistle a Tune—Divide into two groups—boy/girl partners, for instance. Boys and girls line up opposite each other about twenty yards apart. Each girl has pencil and paper. On the signal, the boys race to their partners, whistle a tune, each girl writes down the name of her partner's tune, and the boys race back. A boy cannot return until his partner has guessed his tune. The first to cross the finish line wins. Change roles for the next race.

Find That Tune—This is a good mixer. As people arrive, each is given the name of a tune. For instance, if there are to be five people per group, prepare five slips of paper with the same tune. When everyone has arrived, people then begin to sing, hum, or whistle their tunes. The object is to find others with the same tune. These groups then stay together for the remainder of the evening as they participate in other games.

Draw That Tune—Divide into several small groups. Each group is supplied a chalk board or easel, a piece of poster board, and a felt-tip marker. Each group chooses an artist. These people gather around the leader, who whispers the name of a song. The artists then return to their groups and draw the tune. The first group to yell the correct answer wins. Set a time limit.

Play That Tune—Divide into groups. Supply each group with a spoon, several bottles, a funnel, and a pitcher of water. Players are to fill the bottles to various depths and attempt to play a tune by tapping the bottles with the spoon. Allow about twenty minutes for practice.

Get-Acquainted Musical Chairs—Arrange chairs in a circle facing out. There should be four fewer chairs than people. The players march around the chairs as the music plays. When the music stops, players vie for the chairs. Those who did not find a chair are to walk around the circle and introduce themselves to those who are seated. Those seated are to repeat the name as each person passes by.

When all four have introduced themselves to everyone, those seated get up and the four sit down. The music begins and players march around the circle as before, until the music stops. Each time, four people will be left standing until everyone has been introduced.

The Farmer in the Dell

1. The farmer in the dell,
   The farmer in the dell.
   Heigh-o, the derry-oh!
   The farmer in the dell.

2. The farmer takes the wife, etc.
3. The wife takes the child, etc.
4. The child takes the nurse, etc.
5. The nurse takes the dog, etc.
6. The dog takes the cat, etc.
7. The cat takes the rat, etc.
8. The rat takes the cheese, etc.
9. The cheese stands alone, etc.

Players join hands and walk around in a circle. The farmer stands at center. As the song indicates, the farmer chooses a partner for a wife. Then each player, in turn, selects another to represent the "child," the "nurse," the "dog," the "cat," the "rat," and the "cheese." During the last verse, all gather around the "cheese" and clap their hands. The "cheese" becomes the "farmer" for the next game.

Did You Ever See a Lassie?

Did you ever see a lassie, a lassie, a lassie;
Did you ever see a lassie do this way and that?
Do this way and that way and this way and that way;
Did you ever see a lassie do this way and that?

Players join hands in a circle, with one player at center, and circle around, singing the first two lines of the song while the center player demonstrates some movement. As they reach the lines beginning "Do this way," the players stop circling, drop hands, and imitate the movements of the center player. The center player may decide to sweep, row, bat, play tennis, shoot a rifle, skate, prance like a horse, bow, skip, swim.

If a girl is at center, the players sing "lassie"; if a boy, "laddie."

Here We Go 'Round the Mulberry Bush

Here we go round the mul - berry bush, The
mul - berry bush, the mul - berry bush; Here we go round the
mul - berry bush, On a cold and frost - y morn - ing.

2. This is the way we wash our clothes,
   Wash our clothes, wash our clothes;
   This is the way we wash our clothes,
   So early Monday morning.
3. This is the way we iron our clothes, etc.,
   So early Tuesday morning.
4. This is the way we mend our clothes, etc.,
   So early Wednesday morning.
5. This is the way we scrub the floor, etc.,
   So early Thursday morning.

6. This is the way we sweep the floor, etc.,
   So early Friday morning.
7. This is the way we mix our bread, etc.,
   So early Saturday morning.
8. This is the way we go to church, etc.,
   So early Sunday morning.
9. This is the way we saw our wood, etc.,
   So early in the morning.
10. This is the way we milk the cows, etc.
11. This is the way we mow the lawn, etc.

Players join hands and skip around in a circle while singing the first verse. At the last line, they release hands, whirl around several times, and face the center again. In each succeeding stanza, the players imitate the actions indicated in the song.

London Bridge

1. London Bridge is falling down,
   Falling down, falling down;
   London Bridge is falling down,
   My fair lady.
2. Build it up with iron bars, etc.
3. Iron bars will rust away, etc.
4. Build it up with pins and needles, etc.

5. Pins and needles break and bend, etc.
6. Build it up with penny loaves, etc.
7. Penny loaves will tumble down, etc.
8. Build it up with bricks and mortar, etc.
9. Bricks and mortar wear away, etc.
10. Build it up with gold and silver, etc.
11. Gold and silver will be stolen, etc.
12. We will set a man to watch, etc.
13. Suppose the man should fall asleep, etc.
14. We will set a dog to bark, etc.
15. Here's a prisoner I have got, etc.
16. What's the prisoner done to you, etc.
17. Stole my watch and broke my chain, etc.
18. What'll you take to set him free, etc.
19. One hundred pounds to set him free, etc.
20. One hundred pounds we have not got, etc.
21. Then off to prison you must go, etc.

Two players hold their joined hands as high as they can, forming an arch that represents the bridge. Each of these two players has secretly chosen some object to represent—a rose or a lily, a pearl or a diamond, a golden crown or silver slippers. If they desire they may choose to be animals or birds. The two players agree between them what they are to represent, but do not let the other players know.

The children march around in a circle and through the arch as they sing. On "my fair lady" the bridge comes down on some player. The two children forming the bridge take the captive aside and whisper, "Which would you rather be, a lily or a rose?" The child makes a choice and does not know until then which of the two children is what. The player then stands behind the one chosen. The game continues until each child has chosen and ends with a tug of war between the two teams.

Go In and Out the Windows

1. Go round and round the village,
   Go round and round the village,
   Go round and round the village,
   As we have done before.

2. Go in and out the windows, etc.,
   As we have done before.
3. Now stand and face your partner, etc.,
   And bow before you go.
4. Now follow me to London, etc.,
   As we have done before.

Players stand in a circle, holding hands, as they represent houses in a village. One player remains outside and skips around the circle during the singing of the first stanza. As they sing the second stanza, players in the circle raise their arms so that the runner can go in and out of the circle between them.

The runner remains inside the circle and chooses a partner while the group sings the third stanza. On the last line, the runner bows to the partner. During the singing of the fourth stanza, the runner takes the partner by the hand, they leave the circle and skip around outside. The runner then finds a place within the circle, and the partner becomes the runner for the next game.

Ten Little Indians

1. One little, two little, three little Indians,
   Four little, five little, six little Indians,
   Seven little, eight little, nine little Indians,
   Ten little Indian boys.

2. Ten little, nine little, eight little Indians,
   Seven little, six little, five little Indians,
   Four little, three little, two little Indians,
   One little Indian boy.

Ten players are chosen. As the rest of the group sings the first verse, the Indians run out one at a time. By the end of the first stanza, all are dancing, Indian style, in a circle.

During the second stanza, the Indians drop out one by one until all have disappeared. If there are enough players, two or three circles can be formed.

Pease Porridge Hot

Pease porridge hot, pease porridge cold,
Pease porridge in the pot, nine days old;
Some like it hot, some like it cold,
Some like it in the pot, nine days old.

Players form two concentric circles. The players of the inner circle face those in the outer circle so that each player has a partner.

During the first line of the stanza, each player claps hands on thighs, then claps own hands together, and then claps both hands against the hands of partner, repeating these movements to finish the line.

During the second line, each player claps own thighs with both hands, claps hands together, claps partner's right hand with own right hand, claps own hands together, claps partner's left with own left, claps own together, then claps both hands against partner's hands.

While singing the third and fourth lines, players repeat all these actions from the beginning.

The chorus should then be sung with "La-la-la" or "Dum-dum-dum." While singing, the respective partners join hands and, raising them on a level with their heads, take sixteen skipping, hopping, or sliding steps around the circle to the left, then turn and take the same number of steps around the circle to the right.

As the chorus ends, members of both circles, still facing, move two steps to the left and take new partners, with whom they repeat the song and its motions from the beginning.

ACTION SONGS

Action songs are similar to musical games. The directions are clear, but it requires practice to lead a group in the movements.

Bingo

American Folk Song

Action: Instead of singing "B" in "B-I-N-G-O," clap hands. Clap an additional letter with each repetition until the entire word is clapped instead of sung.

Do Your Ears Hang Low?

Traditional

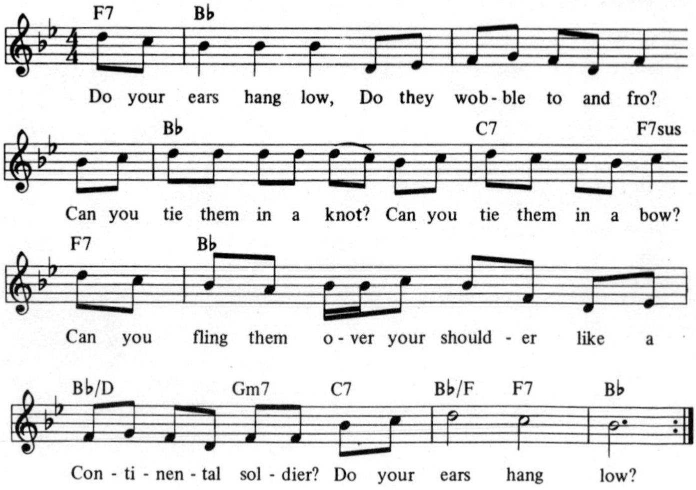
F7 Bb
Do your ears hang low, Do they wob-ble to and fro?
Bb C7 F7sus
Can you tie them in a knot? Can you tie them in a bow?
F7 Bb
Can you fling them o-ver your should-er like a
Bb/D Gm7 C7 Bb/F F7 Bb
Con-ti-nen-tal sol-dier? Do your ears hang low?

2. Do your ears flip, flop,
 Can you use them for a mop?
 Are they stringy at the bottom?
 Are they curly on the top?
 Can you use them for a swatter,
 Can you use them for a blotter?
 Do your ears flip, flop?

Action:

"Do your ears hang low"—Droop hands next to ears.
"Do they wobble to and fro"—Wiggle hand next to ears.
"Can you tie them in a knot"—Imitate tying a knot.
"Can you tie them in a bow"—Imitate shape of a bow.
"Can you fling them over your shoulder"—Imitate shoveling motion over shoulder.
"Do your ears hang low"—Droop hands alongside ears.
"Do your ears flip, flop"—Make flapping motion next to ears.

"Can you use them for a mop"—Imitate mopping floor.
"Are they stringy at the bottom"—Wiggle fingers beside ears.
"Are they curly at the top"—Pretend to fluff top of ears.
"Can you use them for a swatter"—Make swatting motion.
"Can you use them for a blotter"—Pretend to blot, using both hands.
"Do your ears flip, flop"—Make flapping motion.

The Hokey Pokey

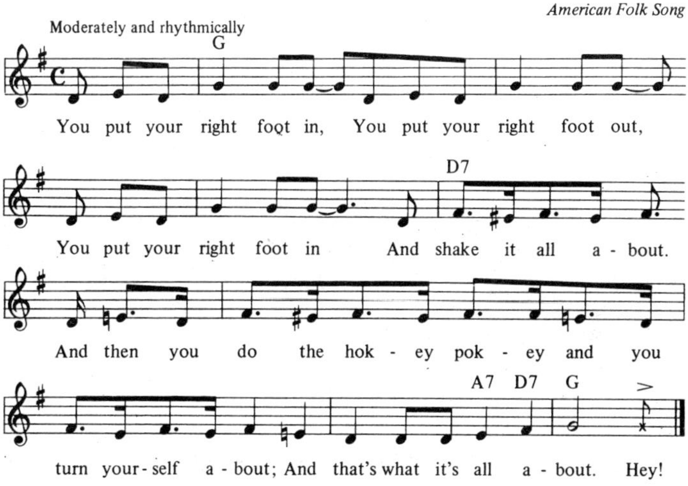
American Folk Song
Moderately and rhythmically
G
You put your right foot in, You put your right foot out,
D7
You put your right foot in And shake it all a - bout.
And then you do the hok - ey pok - ey and you
A7 D7 G
turn your-self a - bout; And that's what it's all a - bout. Hey!

2. You put your left foot in, etc.
3. Right hand, etc.
4. Left hand, etc.
5. Right shoulder, etc.
6. Left shoulder, etc.
7. Right hip, etc.
8. Left hip, etc.
9. Whole self, etc.

Action: Form a circle and follow the instructions.

In a Cabin in a Wood

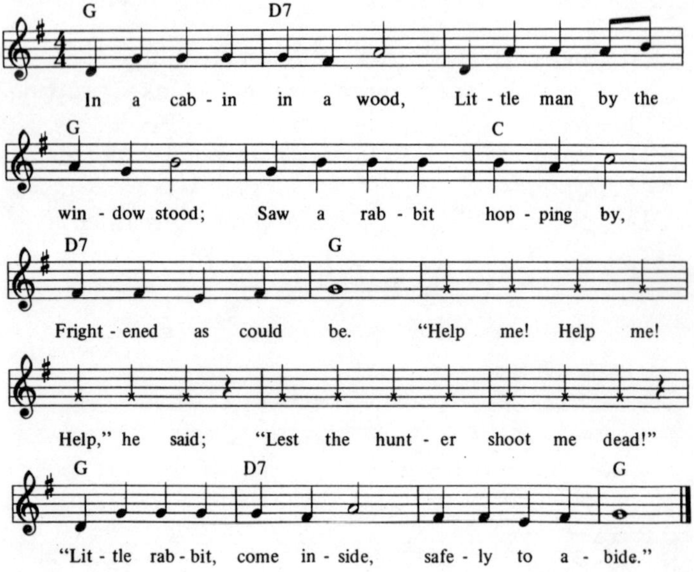

Action:

"In a cabin in a wood"—Form pointed roof with fingers of both hands together.

"Little man by the window stood"—Make binoculars with hands held to eyes.

"Saw a rabbit hopping by"—Make rabbit ears with index and middle fingers; hop him along in rhythm.

"Frightened as could be"—Shake with fear.

"Help me! Help me!"—Shout words in high falsetto; throw hands high on each "Help!"

"Lest the hunter shoot me dead!"—Shoot with forefinger and thumb on each syllable.

"Little rabbit, come inside"—Beckon four times.

"Safely to abide"—Stroke rabbit three times.

Sing once with motions. Then omit a phrase each time until entire song is done in pantomime.

It's Love

2. It's cats, it's cats, it's cats that make the dogs go round, etc.
3. It's girls, it's girls, it's girls that make the boys go round, etc.
4. It's love, it's love, it's love that makes the world go round, etc.

Action: On the chorus, singers sway left and right.

John Brown's Baby

Attributed to William Steffe

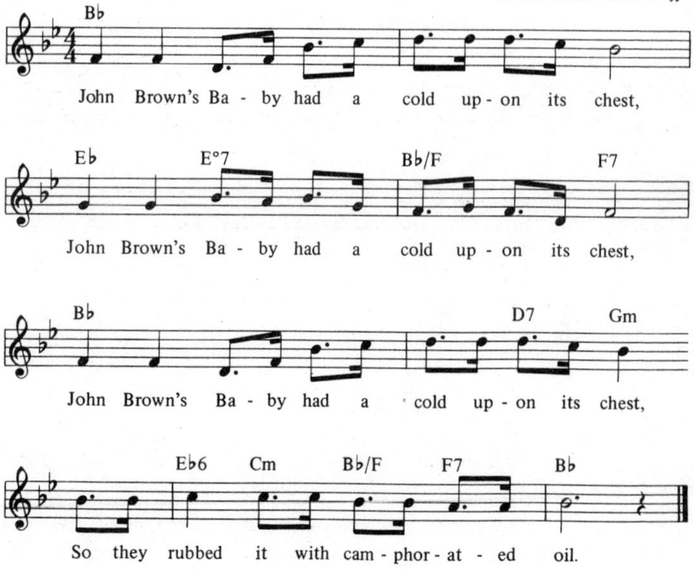
Bb
John Brown's Ba - by had a cold up - on its chest,
Eb E°7 Bb/F F7
John Brown's Ba - by had a cold up - on its chest,
Bb D7 Gm
John Brown's Ba - by had a cold up - on its chest,
Eb6 Cm Bb/F F7 Bb
So they rubbed it with cam - phor - at - ed oil.

Action: Sing the song through six times. With each stanza, add an action in the place of a word.

1. Sing as written.
2. Omit "Baby"—Substitute a rocking motion as though rocking a baby.
3. Omit "cold"—Substitute a little cough.
4. Omit "chest"—Tap chest with open hand.
5. Omit "rubbed"—Gently rub chest.
6. Omit "camphorated oil"—Substitute a little sniff.

Mistress Shady

Bb Eb Cm
Oh, Mis - tress Sha - dy, She is a la - dy,
F7 Bb
She has a daugh - ter Whom I a - dore;
F7 Bb Eb Cm
Each night I court her, I mean the daugh - ter,
Bb F7 Bb Eb
Ev - 'ry Sun - day, Mon - day, Tues - day, Wed - nes-day,
F7 Bb F7 Bb
Thurs - day, Fri - day, Sat - ur - day, Sun - day
F7 Bb F7 Bb
af - ter - noon at half past four.

Action: Divide the group into seven sections and name one for each day of the week. If in rows, name the first row "Sunday," the second, "Monday," etc. All the days of the week should be sung in one breath. Everybody sings the whole song, but as a certain day of the week is sung, that section jumps up and sits down again immediately. On the next singing, add a week. Some groups will enjoy continuing up to five weeks, but a deep breath and faster tempo will be needed.

My Hand on Myself

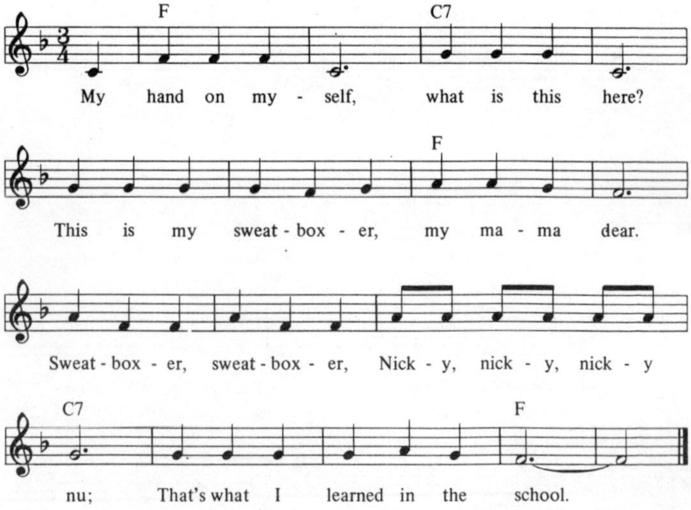

2. This is my eyeblinker, my mama dear.
   Eyeblinker, sweatboxer, nicky, nicky, nicky nu, etc.
3. This is my noseblower, my mama dear.
   Noseblower, eyeblinker, sweatboxer, nicky, nicky, etc.

Action: Point to the head for "sweatboxer." For the verses that follow, substitute one of the following terms for a part of the body, point to it, then repeat all terms in reverse order: Meal-pusher, chin-chopper, neck-stretcher, chest-protector, bread-basket, knee-bender (or baby-sitter), toe-stubber.

Row, Row, Row Your Boat

Traditional American Round

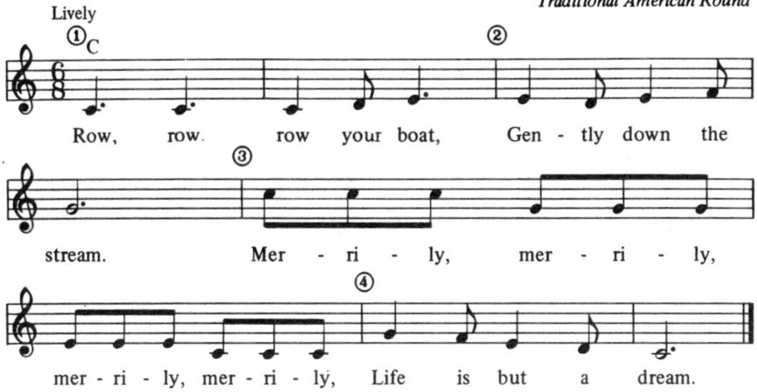
Lively
①C
②
Row, row, row your boat, Gen - tly down the
③
stream. Mer - ri - ly, mer - ri - ly,
④
mer - ri - ly, mer - ri - ly, Life is but a dream.

Action:

"Row, row, row"—Pretend to row a boat.

"Gently down the stream"—Stretch hands straight out, palms down, waving them like ripples in a stream.

"Merrily, merrily, merrily, merrily"—Stand up, place right index finger on top of head and turn completely around.

"Life is but a dream"—Sit down, bring both hands to face, place on cheek as if asleep.

Variations:

(a) Sing as a round with above motions.

(b) Divide crowd by birth months, three months to a group. Each group then sings the song three times with motions.

(c) First, sing the song all the way through. Sing it again, using motions, and leave off "Life is but a dream." Then sing it, leaving off "Merrily, merrily, merrily, merrily, life is but a dream." Next, leave off "Gently down the stream, merrily, etc." Last, sing it with no words (just motions).

(d) Begin by singing only the first word, "Row," and using motions. Begin again, adding the second "row." Continue by starting over each time and adding one word. This can also be done by leaving off the last word each time until only one word is left.

One Finger, One Thumb

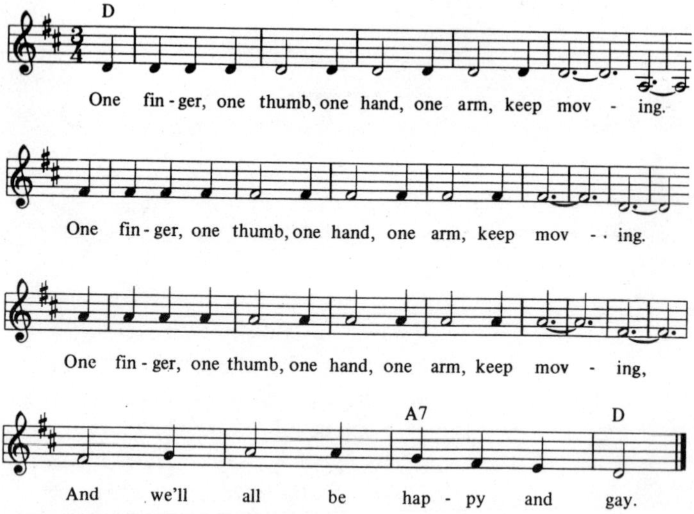
D
One fin - ger, one thumb, one hand, one arm, keep mov - ing.
One fin - ger, one thumb, one hand, one arm, keep mov - - ing.
One fin - ger, one thumb, one hand, one arm, keep mov - ing,
A7
D
And we'll all be hap - py and gay.

2. One finger, one thumb, one hand, one arm, two arms, etc.
3. One finger, one thumb, one hand, one arm, two arms, one leg, etc.
4. One finger, one thumb, one hand, one arm, two arms, one leg, two legs, etc.
5. One finger, one thumb, one hand, one arm, two arms, one leg, two legs, stand up-sit down, etc.

Action: The additional words are to be added three times in each stanza. Keep song in steady rhythm. Accompany the words with appropriate finger, thumb, hand, arm, leg, and standing-and-sitting-down actions.

Three Blue Pigeons

Unknown

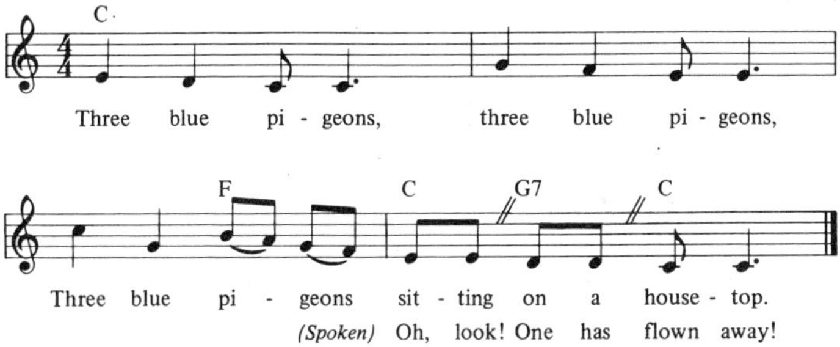
C
Three blue pi - geons, three blue pi - geons,
F C G7 C
Three blue pi - geons sit - ting on a house - top.
(Spoken) Oh, look! One has flown away!

2. Two blue pigeons, etc.
   (*Spoken*) And another flew away!
3. One blue pigeon, etc.
   (*Spoken*) And the last one flew away! Oh-h-h-h-h!
4. No blue pigeon, etc.
   (*Spoken*) Then one came back!
5. One blue pigeon, etc.
   (*Spoken*) Then another came back!
6. Two blue pigeons, etc.
   (*Spoken*) Now the last one has come back!
7. Three blue pigeons, etc.
   (*Spoken*) Hooray!

Action: Leader holds up one, two, or three fingers as spoken lines are pronounced. Whole group shouts "Hooray!" May also be sung to tune of "Three Blind Mice."

Under the Spreading Chestnut Tree

Unknown

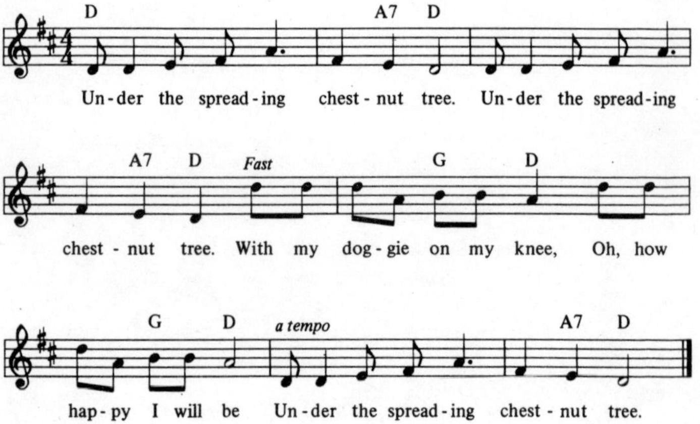

D
A7 D
Un-der the spread-ing chest-nut tree. Un-der the spread-ing
A7 D
Fast
G D
chest - nut tree. With my dog-gie on my knee, Oh, how
G D
a tempo
A7 D
hap-py I will be Un-der the spread-ing chest - nut tree.

Action:

"Under"—Cup hands together low in front of body.
"spreading"—Spread hands outward.
"chest"—Touch chest with both hands.
"-nut"—Touch forehead with both hands.
"tree"—Raise arms over head.
"With my doggie on my knee"—Slap both hands on left knee.

First, sing the song through with the suggested actions. Continue to sing, leaving off one section of words each time, until the song is being done entirely in pantomime.

Way Up in the Sky

Unknown

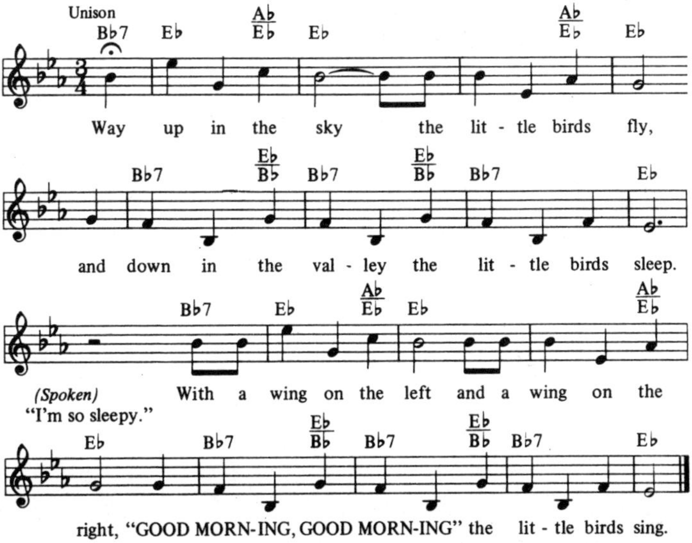
Unison
B♭7 E♭ A♭/E♭ E♭ A♭/E♭ E♭
Way up in the sky the lit - tle birds fly,
B♭7 E♭/B♭ B♭7 E♭/B♭ B♭7 E♭
and down in the val - ley the lit - tle birds sleep.
B♭7 E♭ A♭/E♭ E♭ A♭/E♭
(Spoken) "I'm so sleepy."
With a wing on the left and a wing on the
E♭ B♭7 E♭/B♭ B♭7 E♭/B♭ B♭7 E♭
right, "GOOD MORN-ING, GOOD MORN-ING" the lit - tle birds sing.

Action:

"Way up in the sky"—Swing hands up high and clap once.

"the little birds fly"—Wave arms like wings.

"down in the valley"—Clasp hands loosely, swing them in front of body.

"sleep"—Bring hands up to face and place on cheek as if asleep.

"I'm so sleepy"—Speak in very sleepy manner with eyes closed.

"With a wing on the left"—Swing left arm violently in a circle, flapping hand, then tuck hand under left armpit like a wing.

"a wing on the right"—Do the same with the right arm and hand.

"Good Morning"—Shout out words boisterously and flap arms like wings.

The Teensy-Weensy Spider

Traditional
D A7 D
Oh, the teen - sy - ween - sy spi - der climbed up the wa - ter spout.
D F#m Em7 A7 D
Down came the rain and washed the spi - der out!
D A7 D
Out came the sun and dried up all the rain, And the
D A7 D
teen - sy - ween - sy spi - der climbed up the spout a - gain!

Action:

First line: Simulate spider crawling by joining index finger of one hand to thumb of other, then index finger of second to thumb of first, etc.

Second line: Simulate rain coming down with fingers, then give sweeping motion with arms.

Third line: Form arc above head with arms, then move fingers as if playing piano.

Fourth line: Simulate spider again.

Who Did?

*Seventh chord to modulate up one-half step.

Action: Divide into four groups. On 1, groups jump to feet successively. On 2, groups sit, but in reverse order. On 3, all sit quickly.

OLD FAVORITES

School Days

Will D. Cobb

Gus Edwards, 1907

Bb F7 Bb Bbdim Db F7
School days, school days, dear old Gold - en Rule days;
Read - ing and writ - ing and 'rith - ma - tic,
Bb
Taught to the tune of a hick - 'ry stick;
G7 C7
You were my queen in cal - i - co,
F7 Bb
I was your bash - ful bare - foot beau,
Eb E dim Bb D7
And you wrote on my slate, "I love you, Joe,"
C7 F7 Bb
When we were a cou - ple of kids.

Red River Valley

Cowboy song

G D7 G
From this val - ley they say you are go - ing;
E7 A D7
I will miss your bright eyes and sweet smile,
G G7 C
For they say you are tak' - ing the sun - shine
C♯dim G/D D7 G D.S.
That bright - ened our path - way a - while.

Refrain (same tune as verse):
Come and sit by my side if you love me.
Do not hasten to bid me adieu,
But remember the Red River Valley,
And the cowboy who loved you so true.

2. I have promised you, darling, that never
Shall the words from my lips cause you pain,
And I swear I will love you forever
If you only will love me again.
(*Refrain*)

3. As you go to your home by the ocean,
May you never forget those sweet hours
That we spent in the Red River Valley,
And the love we exchanged 'mid the flowers.
(*Refrain*)

This melody is based on "In the Bright Mohawk Valley" by James Kerrigan, a song popular in New York state in the late nineteenth century.

Old Woman

Traditional American

Men
F
C7
F
Old wom - an, old wom - an, Won't you card my wool for me?
Women
F
C7
F
Speak a lit - tle loud - er, sir, I'm so hard of hear - ing;

2. *Men:* Old woman, old woman,
Won't you darn my socks for me?
Women: Speak a little louder, sir,
I can hardly hear you.

3. *Men:* Old woman, old woman,
Won't you let me court you?
Women: Speak a little louder, sir,
I can almost hear you.

4. *Men:* Old woman, old woman,
Won't you let me marry you?
Women: (clapping hands): Goodness gracious sakes alive!
Now I really hear you.

Bill Bailey

Hughie Cannon, 1902

Moderately fast
F
"Won't you come home, Bill Bail - ey, Won't you come home?"
F♯°7 C7
She cries the whole night long.
C7
"I'll do the cook - ing, hon - ey, I'll pay the rent.
E7 F
I know I've done you wrong.
Re - mem - ber that rain - y eve - ning I drove you out,
F7 B♭
with noth - ing but a fine - tooth comb?
B♭ B♭m F D7
I know I'm to blame; Now ain't that a shame?
G7 C7 F
Bill Bail - ey, won't you please come home?"

A Bicycle Built for Two

Henry Dacre, 1892

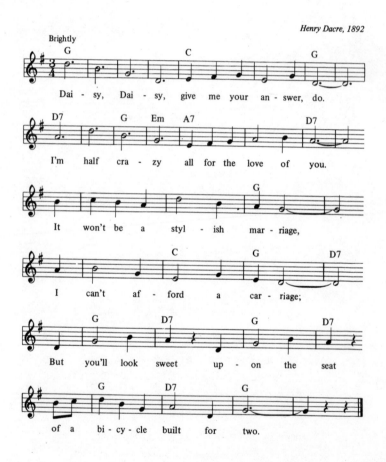

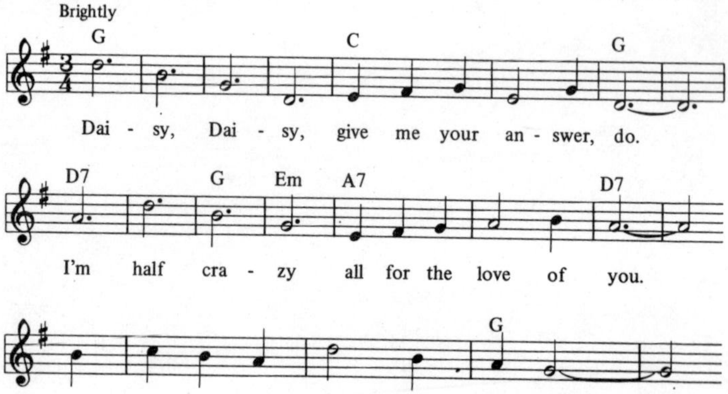
Brightly
G C G
Dai - sy, Dai - sy, give me your an - swer, do.
D7 G Em A7 D7
I'm half cra - zy all for the love of you.
G
It won't be a styl - ish mar - riage,
C G D7
I can't af - ford a car - riage;
G D7 G D7
But you'll look sweet up - on the seat
G D7 G
of a bi - cy - cle built for two.

Six Little Ducks

Traditional American

Moderately fast
F C7
Six lit - tle ducks that I once knew,
F
Fat ones, skin - ny ones, cute ones, too. But the
C7
one lit - tle duck with a feath - er in his back,
C7 F
He ruled the oth - ers with a quack, quack, quack; quack, quack, quack.
C7 F
He ruled the oth - ers with a quack, quack, quack; quack, quack, quack.

2. Down to the river they would go,
Wibble, wabble, wibble, wabble, to and fro.
But the one little duck with a feather in his back,
He ruled the others with a slap, slap, slap.
He ruled the others with a slap, slap, slap.

3. Home from the river they would come,
Wibble, wabble, wibble, wabble, ho-um-hum.
But the one little duck with a feather in his back,
He led the others with a quack, quack, quack.
He led the others with a quack, quack, quack.

My Bonnie Lies Over the Ocean

Scottish Folk Song

2. Last night as I lay on my pillow,
Last night as I lay on my bed,
Last night as I lay on my pillow,
I dream'd that my bonnie was dead.
(*Refrain*)

3. O blow, ye winds, over the ocean,
   And blow, ye winds, over the sea;
   O blow, ye winds, over the ocean,
   And bring back my bonnie to me.
   (*Refrain*)

The Sidewalks of New York
(East Side, West Side)

James W. Blake, 1894 *Charles B. Lawlor, 1894*

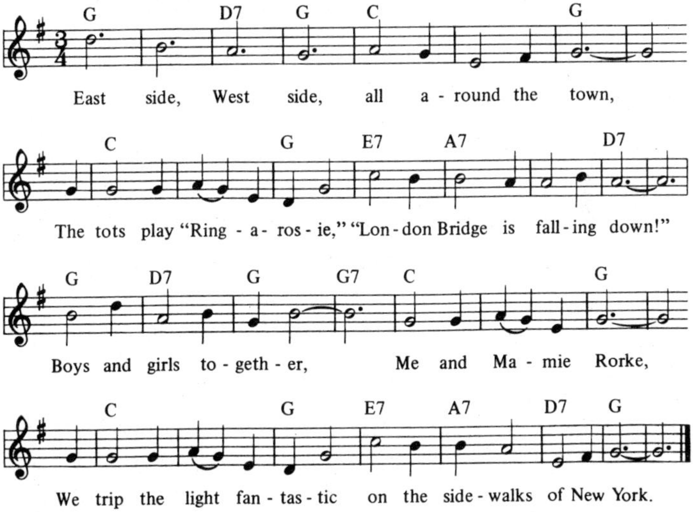
G D7 G C G
East side, West side, all a - round the town,
C G E7 A7 D7
The tots play "Ring - a - ros - ie," "Lon - don Bridge is fall - ing down!"
G D7 G G7 C G
Boys and girls to - geth - er, Me and Ma - mie Rorke,
C G E7 A7 D7 G
We trip the light fan - tas - tic on the side - walks of New York.

Wait for the Wagon

R. Bishop Buckley, 1851

Lively
Bb
Will you come with me, my Phyl - lis dear, To
F7 Bb
yon blue moun - tain free? Where the blos - soms smell the
Eb F7 Bb
sweet - est, Come rove a - long with me. It's
F7 Bb
ev - ery Sun - day morn - ing, When I am by your side,
Eb F7 Bb
We'll jump in - to the wag - on, And we'll all take a ride.
(Refrain)
Bb Eb
Wait for the wa - gon, wait for the wa - gon,
Bb Eb F7 Bb
O wait for the wa - gon, and we'll all take a ride.

2. Where the river runs like silver
And the birds they sing so sweet,
I have a cabin, Phyllis,
And something good to eat.
Come listen to my story;
It will delight your heart.
So jump into the wagon,
And off we will start.
(*Refrain*)

3. Do you believe, my Phyllis, dear,
Old Mike with all his wealth,
Can make you half so happy
As I, with youth and health?
We'll have a little farm,
A horse, a pig, and cow;
And you will mind the dairy,
While I do guide the plough.
(*Refrain*)

4. Your lips are red as poppies,
Your hair so slick and neat,
All braided up with dahlias,
And hollyhocks so sweet.
It's every Sunday morning,
When I am by your side,
We'll jump into the wagon,
And all take a ride.
(*Refrain*)

5. Together, on life's journey,
We'll travel till we stop,
And if we have no trouble,
We'll reach the happy top;
Then come with me, sweet Phyllis,
My dear, my lovely bride,
We'll jump into the wagon,
And all take a ride.
(*Refrain*)

All Through the Night

Attributed to David Owen

Welsh Air: "Ar Hyd y Nos"

F F/A B♭ G C
Sleep my child, and peace at - tend thee
G C B♭ Gm7 C7 F
vig - il keep - ing, All through the night.
B♭ Gm7 C7 F F B♭
All through the night; Guard - ian an - gels
G C B♭ Gm7 C7 F
God will send thee All through the night.
C7 F/C C7 F/C C7 F/C C7 F/C C7 F/C C Dm
Soft the drow - sy hours are creep - ing, Hill and vale in
G7 B♭/C C7 F B♭
slum - ber steep - ing, I my lov - ing

2. While the moon her watch is keeping
All through the night;
While the weary world is sleeping
All through the night.
O'er thy spirit gently stealing,
Visions of delight revealing,
Breathes a pure and holy feeling,
All through the night.

The Crawdad Song

Anonymous — *American Negro Folk Song*

Moderately fast
F
You get a line and I'll get a pole, hon - ey.
C7
You get a line and I'll get a pole, babe.
F
You get a line and I'll get a pole;
B♭ F C7 F
We'll go down to the craw-dad hole, hon-ey, ba - by mine.

2. Yonder is a man with a pack on his back, honey,
   Yonder is a man with a pack on his back, babe,
   Yonder is a man with a pack on his back,
   Totin' all the crawdads he can pack,
   Honey, baby mine.

3. A-settin' on the ice till my feet got hot, honey, etc.,
   A-watchin' that crawdad rack and trot,
   Honey, baby mine.

4. Whatcha gonna do when the lake runs dry, honey, etc.,
   Sit on the bank and watch the crawdads die,
   Honey, baby mine.

5. Whatcha gonna do when your man goes away, honey,
   etc.,
   Get me a better one very next day,
   Honey, baby mine.

There Was an Old Woman

American Folk Song

Moderately
G
1. There was an old wo - man who swal - lowed a fly.
Am D7 G
I don't know why she swal - lowed a fly. Per - haps she'll die.
G
2. There was an old wo - man who swal - lowed a spi - der, who
Am D7
wrig - gled and jig - gled and tic - kled in - side her. She
G
swal - lowed the spi - der to catch the fly. And
Am D7 G
I don't know why she swal - lowed a fly. Per - haps she'll die.
G
3. There was an old wo - man who swal - lowed a bird.
Guitar tacet D7 G
(Spoken) How ab - surd! To swal - low a bird. She swal - lowed the bird to
Am D7
catch the spi - der that wrig - gled and jig - gled and tic - kled in - side her. She

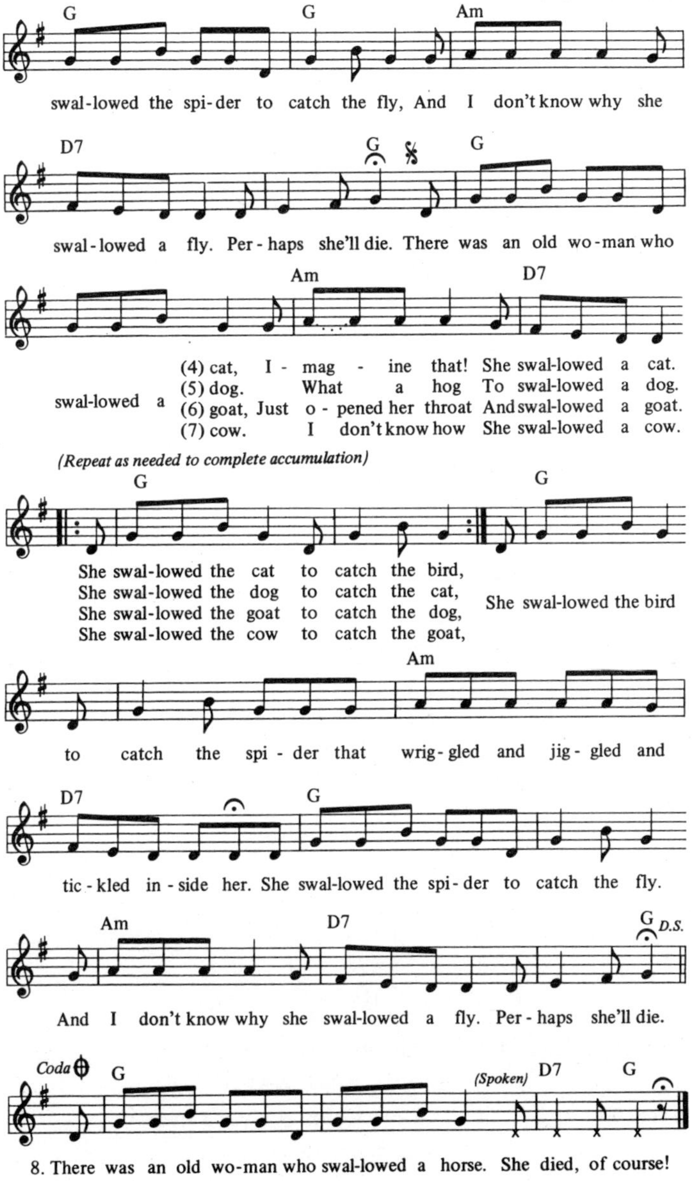
G G Am
swal-lowed the spi-der to catch the fly, And I don't know why she
D7 G G
swal-lowed a fly. Per-haps she'll die. There was an old wo-man who
Am D7
swal-lowed a
(4) cat, I - mag - ine that! She swal-lowed a cat.
(5) dog. What a hog To swal-lowed a dog.
(6) goat, Just o - pened her throat And swal-lowed a goat.
(7) cow. I don't know how She swal-lowed a cow.
(Repeat as needed to complete accumulation)
G G
She swal-lowed the cat to catch the bird,
She swal-lowed the dog to catch the cat,
She swal-lowed the goat to catch the dog,
She swal-lowed the cow to catch the goat,
She swal-lowed the bird
Am
to catch the spi - der that wrig-gled and jig-gled and
D7 G
tic-kled in-side her. She swal-lowed the spi-der to catch the fly.
Am D7 G D.S.
And I don't know why she swal-lowed a fly. Per-haps she'll die.
Coda G (Spoken) D7 G
8. There was an old wo-man who swal-lowed a horse. She died, of course!

On Top of Old Smoky

American Folk Song

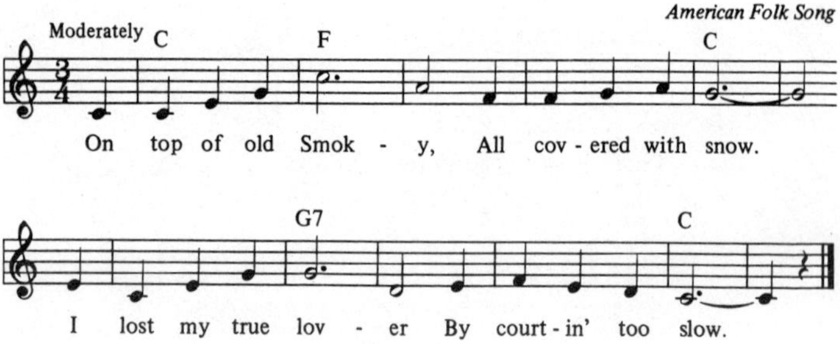
Moderately
C
F
C
On top of old Smok - y, All cov - ered with snow.
G7
C
I lost my true lov - er By court - in' too slow.

2. Now, courting's a pleasure,
   Parting is grief;
   But a false-hearted lover
   Is worse than a thief.

3. A thief he will rob you
   And take all you have;
   But a false-hearted lover
   Will lead you to the grave.

4. The grave will decay you
   And turn you to dust,
   There ain't one in a million
   A poor girl (boy) can trust.

5. They'll hug you and kiss you
   And tell you more lies
   Than the crossties on railroads
   Or the stars in the skies.

6. They'll tell you they love you
To give your heart ease;
But the minute your back's turned,
They'll court who they please.

7. I'll go back to old Smoky,
Old Smoky so high,
Where the wild birds and turtledoves
Can hear my sad cry.

8. Bury me on old Smoky,
Old Smoky so high,
Where the wild birds in heaven
Can hear my sad cry.

9. On top of old Smoky
All covered with snow,
I lost my true lover
By courtin' too slow.

Tell Me Why

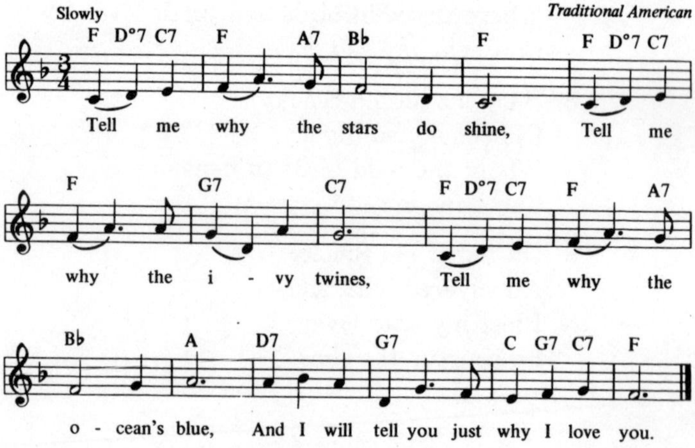

2. Because God made the stars to shine,
Because God made the ivy twine,
Because God made the sky so blue,
Because God made you, that's why I love you.

3. I know it's true that God above,
Wanted someone for me to love.
And he chose you from all the rest,
Because he knew, dear, I'd love you the best.

The Riddle Song

English Folk Song

Slowly
F
B♭
F
I gave my love a cher - ry that has no stone,
C7
F
C7
I gave my love a chick - en that has no bone,
F
C7
I gave my love a ring that has no end,
F
B♭
F
I gave my love a ba - by that's no cry - in'.

2. How can there be a cherry that has no stone?
   How can there be a chicken that has no bone?
   How can there be a ring that has no end?
   How can there be a baby that's no cryin'?

3. A cherry when it's bloomin', it has no stone;
   A chicken when it's pippin', it has no bone;
   A ring when it's a-rollin', it has no end;
   A baby when it's sleepin', it's no cryin'.

Buffalo Gals

Anonymous *Adapted from a tune by Cool White, 1844*

Brightly
(Verse)
C
As I was walk - ing down the street,
G7 C C
Down the street, down the street, A pret - ty girl I
G7 C
chanced to meet, By the light of the sil - very moon. Oh,
(Refrain)
C
Buf - fa - lo gals, won't you come out to - night,
G7 C
Come out to - night, come out to - night? Oh,
C
Buf - fa - lo gals, won't you come out to - night, And
G7 C
dance by the light of the moon?

2. I asked her if she'd stop and talk,
   Stop and talk, stop and talk;
   Her feet took up the whole sidewalk;
   She was fair to view.
   (*Refrain*)

3. I asked her if she'd be my wife,
   Be my wife, be my wife;
   Then I'd be happy all my life,
   If she'd marry me.
   (*Refrain*)

When You Were Sweet Sixteen

James Thornton, 1898

C E F A7/E Dm
I love you as I nev - er loved be - fore,
G7 C C♯°7 G7
Since first I met you on the vil - lage green.
C E F A7/E Dm
Come to me or my dream of love is o'er,
F F♯°7 C
I love you as I loved you When you were
D7 G7 C
sweet, when you were sweet six - teen.

This Old Man

Traditional English

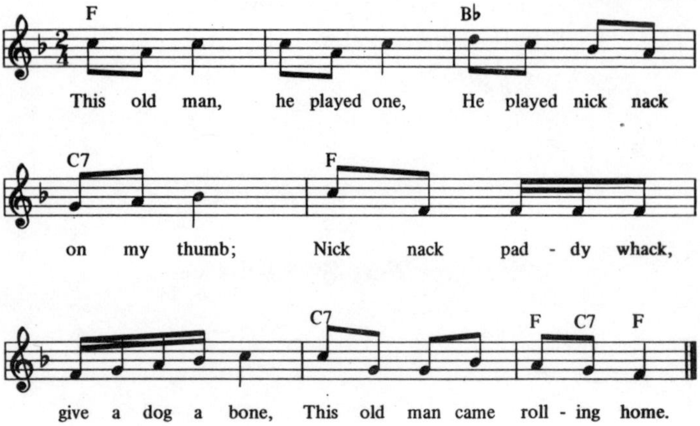
F
Bb
This old man, he played one, He played nick nack
C7
F
on my thumb; Nick nack pad - dy whack,
C7
F C7 F
give a dog a bone, This old man came roll - ing home.

2. This old man, he played two,
   He played nick nack on my shoe, etc.
3. This old man, he played three,
   He played nick nack on my tree, etc.
4. This old man, he played four,
   He played nick nack on my door, etc.
5. This old man, he played five,
   He played nick nack on my hive, etc.
6. This old man, he played six,
   He played nick nack on my sticks, etc.
7. This old man, he played seven,
   He played nick nack on my Devon, etc.
8. This old man, he played eight,
   He played nick nack on my gate, etc.
9. This old man, he played nine,
   He played nick nack on my line, etc.
10. This old man, he played ten,
    He played nick nack on my hen, etc.

Hole in the Bucket

Pennsylvania Dutch Folk Song

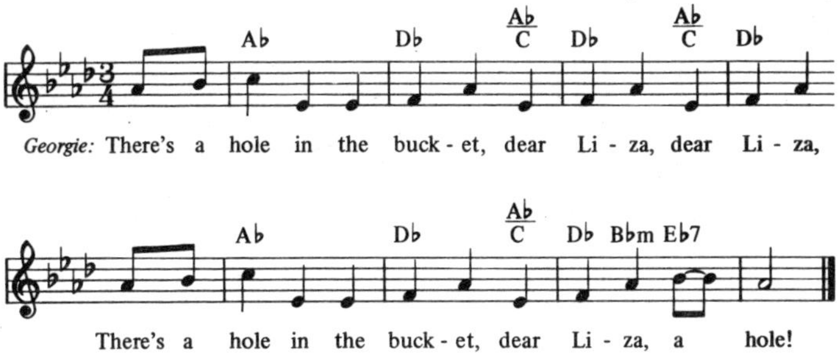
Ab Db Ab/C Db Ab/C Db
Georgie: There's a hole in the buck - et, dear Li - za, dear Li - za,
Ab Db Ab/C Db Bbm Eb7
There's a hole in the buck - et, dear Li - za, a hole!

Liza: Mend the hole, then, dear Georgie, dear Georgie, dear Georgie,
Mend the hole, then, dear Georgie, dear Georgie, mend the hole.

Georgie: With what shall I mend it, dear Liza, etc.
Liza: With a straw, then, dear Georgie, etc.
Georgie: If the straw be too long, dear Liza, etc.
Liza: Cut the straw, then, dear Georgie, etc.

Georgie:	*Liza:*
With what shall I cut it, etc.	With a knife, etc.
If the knife be too dull, etc.	Whet the knife, etc.
With what shall I whet it, etc.	With a stone, etc.
If the stone be too rough, etc.	Smooth the stone, etc.
With what shall I smooth it, etc.	With water, etc.
In what shall I fetch it, etc.	In a bucket, etc.
There's a hole in the bucket, etc.	

Alouette
(Gentle Skylark)

Brightly
French-Canadian Folk Song
G D7 G
A - lou - et - te, gen - tille A - lou - et - te,
D7 G Fine
A - lou - et - te, Je te plu - me - rai.
G D7
Je - te plu - me - rai la tête, Je - te plu - me - rai la tête.
D7 D.C. D D7 G D7
Et la tête, Et la tête! A - lou - ette, A - lou - ette! Oh,

(In stanza 1, "la tête" means *head.*)

2. Alouette, gentille Alouette,
   Alouette, je te plumerai.
   Je te plumerai la bec (beak),
   Je te plumerai le bec.
   Et le bec, et le bec!
   Et la tête, et la tête!
   Alouette, Alouette!
   Oh-h-h-h,

3. Alouette, gentille Alouette,
   Alouette, je te plumerai.
   Je te plumerai les ailes (wings),
   Je te plumerai les ailes.
   Et les ailes, et les ailes!
   Et la tête, et la tête!
   Alouette, Alouette!
   Oh-h-h-h,

4. Le cou (neck)
5. Le dos (back)
6. Les pattes (feet)
7. Le queue (tail)

John Jacob Jingleheimer Schmidt

Traditional
F C7 Gm7 C7
John Ja - cob Jin - gle - hei - mer Schmidt, His name is my name
F C7 F Gm7
too. When - ev - er we go out, the peo - ple al - ways shout,
C7 F C7
repeat as desired
"John Ja - cob Jin - gle - hei - mer Schmidt." Da - da - da - da - da - da - da

Sing through several times, each time singing more softly, except for "Da, da, da . . . ." The last time, sing the words so softly you can barely hear them and shout out "Da, da, da. . . ."

Polly-Wolly-Doodle

American Minstrel

F
Oh, I went down South for to see my Sal;
B♭ F C7
Sing Pol - ly - wol - ly - doo - dle all the day.
My Sal - ly is a spunk - y gal; Sing
F
Pol - ly - wol - ly - doo - dle all the day.
(Refrain)
F
Fare thee well, Fare thee well,
Fare - well, Fare - well,
B♭ F C7
Fare thee well, my fair - y fay, For I'm
goin' to Louis - i - an - na, For to see my Su - sy - an - na, Sing
F
Pol - ly - wol - ly - doo - dle all the day.

2. Oh, my Sal she is a maiden fair;
Sing Polly-wolly-doodle all the day.
With curly eyes and laughing hair;
Sing Polly-wolly-doodle all the day.
(*Refrain*)

3. A grasshopper sitting on a railroad track;
   Sing Polly-wolly-doodle all the day.
   A-pickin' his teeth with a carpet tack;
   Sing Polly-wolly-doodle all the day.
   (*Refrain*)

Shenandoah

American Sea Chantey

Slowly
Eb Bb7 Eb Ab
Oh, Shen - an - doah, I long to hear you, A - way, you roll - ing
Eb Ab B7 Cm
riv - er, Oh, Shen - an - doah, I long to hear you, A -
Eb Eb Bb7 Eb
way, we're bound a - way, 'Cross the wide Mis - sour - i.

2. Oh, Shenandoah's my native valley,
   Away, you rolling river.
   Oh, Shenandoah's my native valley.
   Away, we're bound away
   'Cross the wide Missouri.

3. Oh, Shenandoah, it's far I wander, etc.
4. Oh, Shenandoah has rushing waters, etc.
5. Oh, Shenandoah, I long to see you, etc.
6. Oh, Shenandoah, I love your daughter, etc.
7. Oh, Shenandoah, I'm bound to leave you, etc.
8. Oh, Shenandoah, I'll never grieve you, etc.

Clementine

Attributed to Percy Montrose, 1883

Brightly
F
C7
In a cav - ern, in a can - yon, Ex - ca - va - ting for a mine,
F
C7
F
Lived a min - er, for - ty nin - er, And his daugh - ter, Clem - en - tine.
(Refrain)
F
C7
Oh my darl - ing, oh my darl - ing, Oh my darl - ing Clem - en - tine,
F
C7
F
You are lost and gone for - ev - er, Dread - ful sor - ry, Clem - en - tine.

2. Light she was, and like a fairy,
   And her shoes were number nine,
   Herring boxes without topses,
   Sandals were for Clementine.
   (*Refrain*)

3. Drove she ducklings to the water
   Every morning just at nine,
   Hit her foot against a splinter,
   Fell into the foaming brine.
   (*Refrain*)

4. Ruby lips above the water,
   Blowing bubbles soft and fine,
   But, alas! I was no swimmer,
   So I lost my Clementine.
   (*Refrain*)

5. In a churchyard near the canyon,
Where the myrtle doth entwine,
There grow roses and other posies,
Fertilized by Clementine.
(*Refrain*)

6. In my dreams she still doth haunt me,
Robed in garments soaked with brine;
Though in life I used to hug her,
Now she's dead, I draw the line.
(*Refrain*)

7. Listen Boy Scouts, heed the warning
To this tragic tale of mine:
Artificial respiration
Could have saved my Clementine.
(*Refrain*)

8. How I missed her, how I missed her,
How I missed my Clementine,
Till I kissed her little sister,
And forgot my Clementine.
(*Refrain*)

Blow the Man Down

American Sea Chantey

Briskly
C
I'll sing you a song, a good song of the sea,
A7 Dm G7
To me way, aye, blow the man down;
G7
And trust that you'll join in the cho - rus with me,
C G7 C
Give me some time to blow the man down.

2. 'Twas on board a Black Baller I first served my time,
And away, hey, blow the man down;
And on the Black Baller I wasted my prime.
Give me some time to blow the man down.

3. It's when a Black Baller's preparing for sea,
And away, aye, blow the man down;
You'd split your sides laughing at the sights you would see,
Give me some time to blow the man down.

4. With the tinkers and tailors and soldiers and all,
To me way, aye, blow the man down;
That ship as good seamen on board the Black Ball;
Give me some time to blow the man down.

5. It's when a Black Baller is clear of the land,
And away, hey, blow the man down;
Our bosun then gives us the word of command.
Give me some time to blow the man down.

6. It's larboard and starboard on the deck you will sprawl,
And away, aye, blow the man down;
For "Kicking" Jack Williams commands the Black Ball.
Give me some time to blow the man down.

7. "Lay aft!" is the cry, "To the break of the poop!"
And away, hey, blow the man down;
"Or I'll help you along with the toe of my boot."
Give me some time to blow the man down.

8. Pay attention to orders, yes, you, one and all,
To me way, aye, blow the man down;
For see, right above you, there flies the Black Ball.
Give me some time to blow the man down.

9. It's when a Black Baller comes down to the dock,
And away, hey, blow the man down;
The lasses and lads to the pier-heads do flock.
Give me some time to blow the man down.

The Black Ball Line was a famous line of packet boats that carried mail, passengers, and cargo between New York and Liverpool.

Sipping Cider Through a Straw

Traditional American

The first "ci-" is prolonged to give the impression of a long sip through a straw.

2. I told that girl I didn't see how
   She sipped that ci—der through a straw.
   I told that girl I didn't see how
   She sipped that cider through a straw.

3. Then cheek to cheek, and jaw to jaw,
   We sipped that ci—der through a straw, etc.

4. And now and then the straw would slip,
   And I'd sip ci—der from her lip, etc.

5. And now I've got a mother-in-law,
   From sipping ci—der through a straw, etc.

Down in the Valley
(Prisoner's Song)

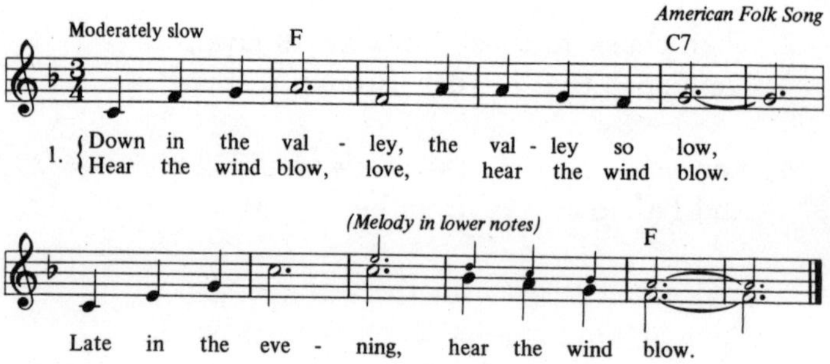

2. If you don't love me, then love who you please,
Throw your arms 'round me, give my heart ease.
Give my heart ease, dear, give my heart ease.
Throw your arms 'round me, give my heart ease.

3. Roses love sunshine, violets love dew;
Angels in heaven know I love you.
Know I love you, dear, know I love you,
Angels in heaven know I love you.

4. Build me a castle forty feet high,
So I can see him as he goes by.
As he goes by, dear, as he goes by,
So I can see him as he goes by.

5. Writing this letter, containing three lines,
Answer my question, "Will you be mine?"
"Will you be mine, dear, will you be mine?"
Answer my question, "Will you be mine?"

6. Send me a letter, send it by mail,
   Send it in care of the Birmingham jail.
   The Birmingham jail, love, the Birmingham jail,
   Send it in care of the Birmingham jail.

7. Down in the valley, the valley so low,
   Late in the evening, hear the train blow.
   Hear the train blow, love, hear the train blow,
   Late in the evening, hear the train blow.

My Name Is Yon Yonson

Traditional

F Bb/F F Bb/F
My name is Yon Yon - son, I come from Vis - con - sin. I
F Dm Gm C7
vork in the lum - ber - yards there. Ven I
Gm C7 Gm C7
valk down the street all the peo - ple I meet say, "Hel -
Gm C7 F
lo, vat's your name?" and I say,

I've Been Working on the Railroad

Lively
Traditional American
G
I've been work - ing on the rail - road,
C/G G
All the live - long day; I've been work - ing on the
A7 D7
rail - road Just to pass the time a - way.
D7 G C
Don't you hear the whis - tle blow - ing, Rise up so ear - ly in the
B7 C G
morn; Don't you hear the cap - tain shout - ing:
C D7 G G
"Di - nah, blow your horn!" Di - nah won't you blow,
C Am D7 1G
Di-nah won't you blow, Di-nah won't you blow your horn;

2 G
horn? Some-one's in the kitch - en with Di - nah,
D7
Some - one's in the kitch - en I know,
G C
Some - one's in the kitch - en with Di - nah,
G/D D7 G
Strum-min' on the old ban - jo. Fee, Fie,
3 3 D7
Fid - dle - ee - i O, Fee, Fie, Fid - dle - ee - i O,
G C 3 G/D D7 G
Fee, Fie, Fid - dle - ee - i O, Strum-min' on the old ban - jo.

Michael Finnigin

Traditional

2. There was an old man named Michael Finnigin,
He went fishing with a pinigin,
Caught a fish but dropped it inigin,
Poor old Michael Finnigin,
Beginigin!

3. There was an old man named Michael Finnigin,
Climbed a tree and barked his shinigin,
Took off several yards of skinigin,
Poor old Michael Finnigin,
Beginigin!

4. There was an old man named Michael Finnigin,
He grew fat and then grew thinigin,
Then he died and had to beginigin,
Poor old Michael Finnigin,
It's the endigin!

Skinney Marinkie Dinkie Dink

American College Song

A♭
Skin-ney Ma-rink-ie dink-ie dink, Skin-ney Ma-rink-ie do,
Fm7 E♭7 B♭m E♭7
I love you, Skin-ney Ma-rink-ie
B♭m E♭7 B♭m E♭7
dink-ie dink, Skin-ney Ma-rink-ie do, I love
A♭
you. I love you in the morn-ing and I
D♭ B♭
love you late at night, I love you in the
E♭7
ev-'ning when the moon is shin-ing bright. Oh,
A♭
Skin-ney Ma-rink-ie dink-ie dink, Skin-ney Ma-rink-ie
E♭7
do, I love you.

ROUNDS

White Coral Bells

Traditional English Round

① B♭ F7 B♭
White cor - al bells up - on a slen - der stalk,
② B♭ F7 B♭
Lil - ies of the val - ley deck my gar - den walk.
③ B♭ F7 B♭
Oh, don't you wish that you could hear them ring?
④ B♭ F7 B♭
That will hap - pen on - ly when the fair - ies sing.

Goose Round

Traditional Round

① D ②
Why should - n't my goose Sing as well as thy goose,
③ ④
When I paid for my goose Twice as much as thou?

O How Lovely Is the Evening

Traditional American Round

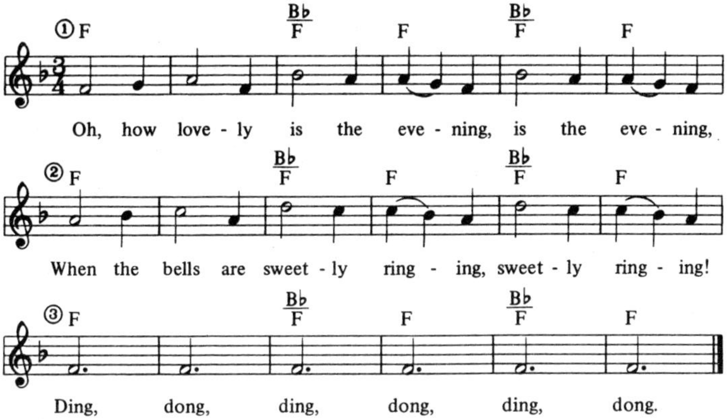
① F Bb/F F Bb/F F
Oh, how love - ly is the eve - ning, is the eve - ning,
② F Bb/F F Bb/F F
When the bells are sweet - ly ring - ing, sweet - ly ring - ing!
③ F Bb/F F Bb/F F
Ding, dong, ding, dong, ding, dong.

Upward Trail

Traditional American Round

① G ② D7
We're on the up - ward trail! We're on the up - ward trail!
G
Sing - ing, sing - ing, ev - 'ry - bod - y sing - ing, As we go!
D7
We're on the up - ward trail! We're on the up - ward trail!
G
Sing - ing, sing - ing, ev - 'ry - bod - y sing - ing, Home - ward bound!

Rejoice in the Lord Alway

From Philippians 4:4

Traditional Round

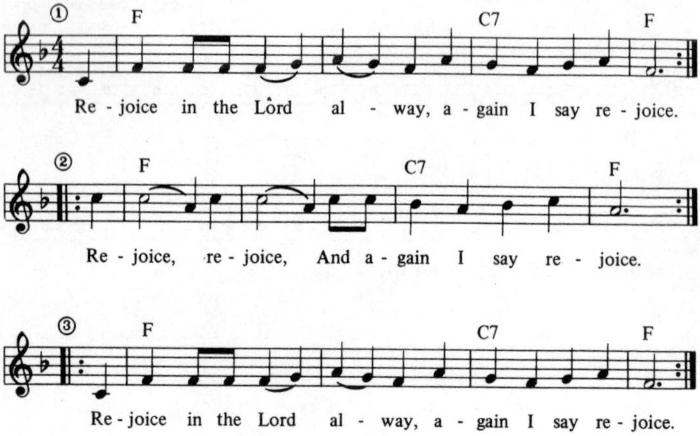
① F C7 F
Re - joice in the Lord al - way, a - gain I say re - joice.
② F C7 F
Re - joice, re - joice, And a - gain I say re - joice.
③ F C7 F
Re - joice in the Lord al - way, a - gain I say re - joice.

Come Follow

Traditional English Round

Brightly

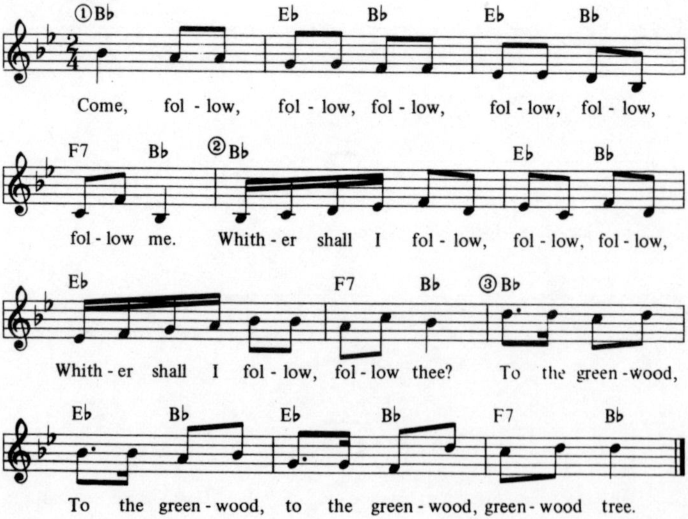
①B♭ E♭ B♭ E♭ B♭
Come, fol - low, fol - low, fol - low, fol - low, fol - low,
F7 B♭ ②B♭ E♭ B♭
fol - low me. Whith - er shall I fol - low, fol - low, fol - low,
E♭ F7 B♭ ③B♭
Whith - er shall I fol - low, fol - low thee? To the green - wood,
E♭ B♭ E♭ B♭ F7 B♭
To the green - wood, to the green - wood, green - wood tree.

Music Alone Shall Live

(Die Musica)

German Canon

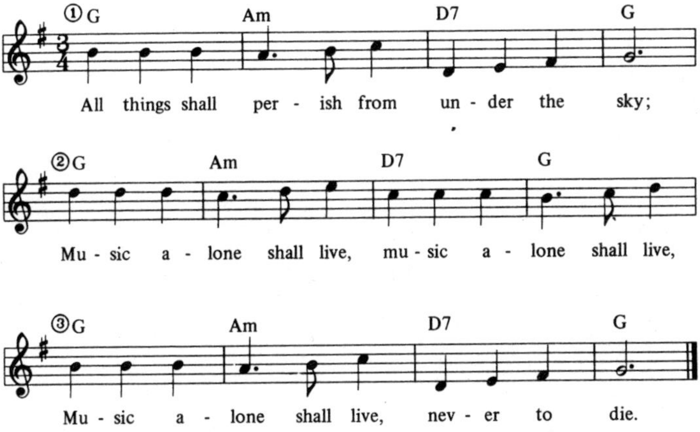
①G Am D7 G
All things shall per - ish from un - der the sky;
②G Am D7 G
Mu - sic a - lone shall live, mu - sic a - lone shall live,
③G Am D7 G
Mu - sic a - lone shall live, nev - er to die.

German version:
Himmel und Erde mussen vergehen;
aber die Musica, aber die Musica,
aber die Musica, bleiben bestehen.

Hey! Ho! Nobody Home

Briskly

Traditional English Round

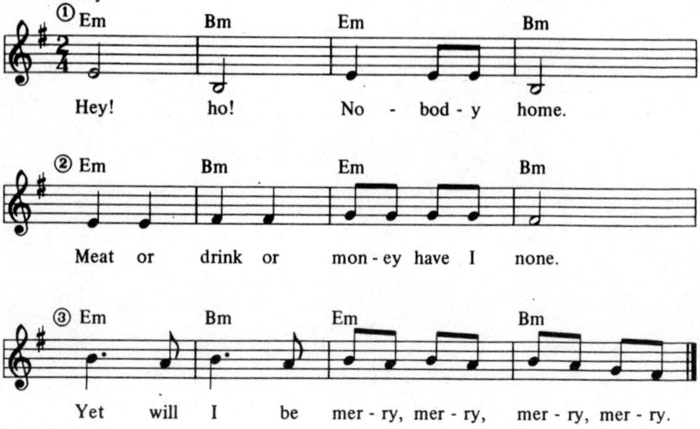

Rose, Rose

Traditional English Round

This round makes a perfect complement to "Hey, Ho, Nobody Home."

Three Blind Mice

Traditional English Round

① C G7 C G7 C
Three blind mice, three blind mice,
② C G7 C G7 C
See how they run, see how they run. They
③ C G7 C
all ran af - ter the far - mer's wife. She
G7 C
cut off their tails with a carv - ing knife. Did you
④ C G7 C G7 C
ev - er see such a sight in your life, as three blind mice?

I Love the Mountains

Hawaiian Folk Song

For Thy Gracious Blessings

Traditional

Kookaburra

Moderately slow

Australian Round

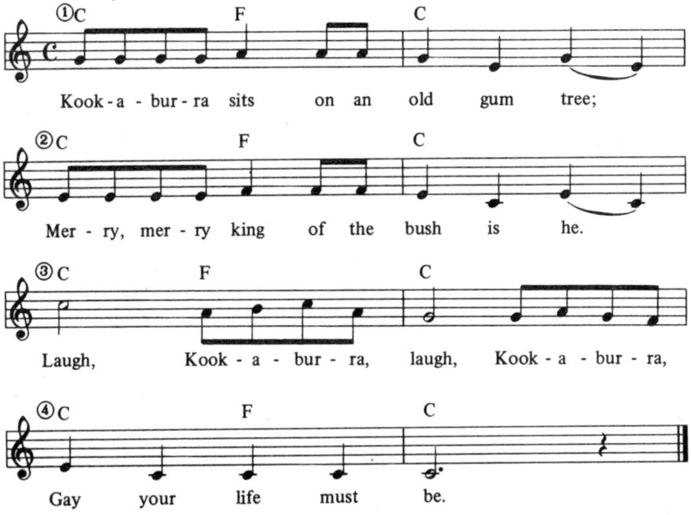
①C F C
Kook-a - bur - ra sits on an old gum tree;
②C F C
Mer - ry, mer - ry king of the bush is he.
③C F C
Laugh, Kook - a - bur - ra, laugh, Kook - a - bur - ra,
④C F C
Gay your life must be.

From *The Ditty Bag,* by Janet E. Tobitt.

Whippoorwill

Traditional American Round

Moderate time

①F C7 F
Gone to bed is the set - ting sun,
②F C7 F
Night is com - ing and day is done; Whip - poor -
③F C7 F
will, whip - poor - will, has just be - gun.

Frère Jacques

English version:

Are you sleeping, are you sleeping,
Brother John, Brother John?
Morning bells are ringing, morning bells are ringing,
Ding, dong, ding; ding, dong, ding.

Spanish version:

Fray Felipe, Fray Felipe,
Duermus tu, duermus tu?
Toca la campana, toca la campana,
Tan, tan, tan; tan, tan, tan.

German version:

Onkel Jakob, Onkel Jakob,
Schlafst du noch, schlafst du noch,
Ringe an der Glocke, ringe an der Glocke,
Bim, bam, bom; bim, bam, bom.

Grant Us Peace, O Lord
(Dona Nobis Pacem)

Unknown

Latin version:
Dona nobis pacem, pacem; dona nobis pacem.
Dona nobis pacem; dona nobis pacem.
Dona nobis pacem; dona nobis pacem.

Tallis Canon

Thomas Ken — Thomas Tallis

①G C D G ② C D G ③
All praise to Thee, my God, this night, For
C D G ④ C D G C D G
all the bless - ings of the light; Keep me, oh, keep me,
C D G C D G C D G
King of kings, Be - neath Thine own al - might - y wings.

O Give Thanks

Traditional

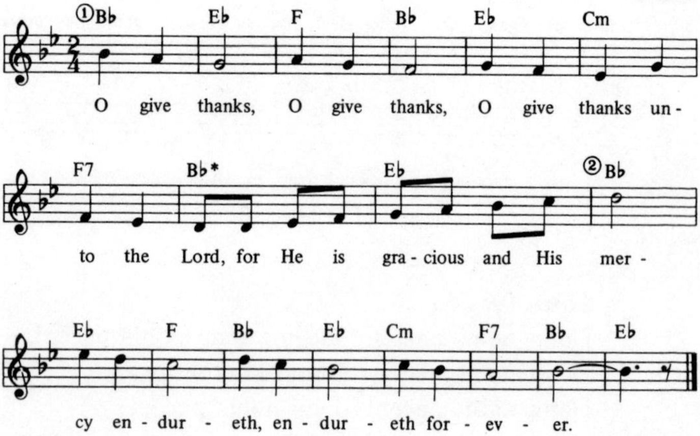
①B♭ E♭ F B♭ E♭ Cm
O give thanks, O give thanks, O give thanks un -
F7 B♭* E♭ ②B♭
to the Lord, for He is gra - cious and His mer -
E♭ F B♭ E♭ Cm F7 B♭ E♭
cy en - dur - eth, en - dur - eth for - ev - er.

*When sung as a round, group 1 sings through once and from the beginning to * again, while second group, beginning at ², sings through once.

SPIRITUALS

Swing Low, Sweet Chariot

American Negro Spiritual

(Refrain)
F
Hum . . . .
Swing low, sweet char - i - ot, Com-in' fo' to car - ry me home,
Dm F/C C7 F Fine
Hum . . . . Hum . . . . .
Swing low, sweet char - i - ot, Com-in' fo' to car - ry me home.
(Verse)
F
I looked o - ver Jor - dan and what did I see,
Com - in' fo' to car - ry me home, A band of an - gels
B♭ F Dm. F/C C7 F
com - in' aft - er me, Com - in' fo' to car - ry me home.

2. If you get there before I do,
   Comin' fo' to carry me home,
   Tell all my friends I'm comin' too,
   Comin' fo' to carry me home.

3. The brightest day that ever I saw,
   Comin' fo' to carry me home,
   When Jesus wash'd my sins away,
   Comin' fo' to carry me home.

4. I'm sometimes up and sometimes down,
   Comin' fo' to carry me home,
   But still my soul feels heav'nly bound,
   Comin' fo' to carry me home.

Dese Bones Gonna' Rise Again

American Negro Spiritual

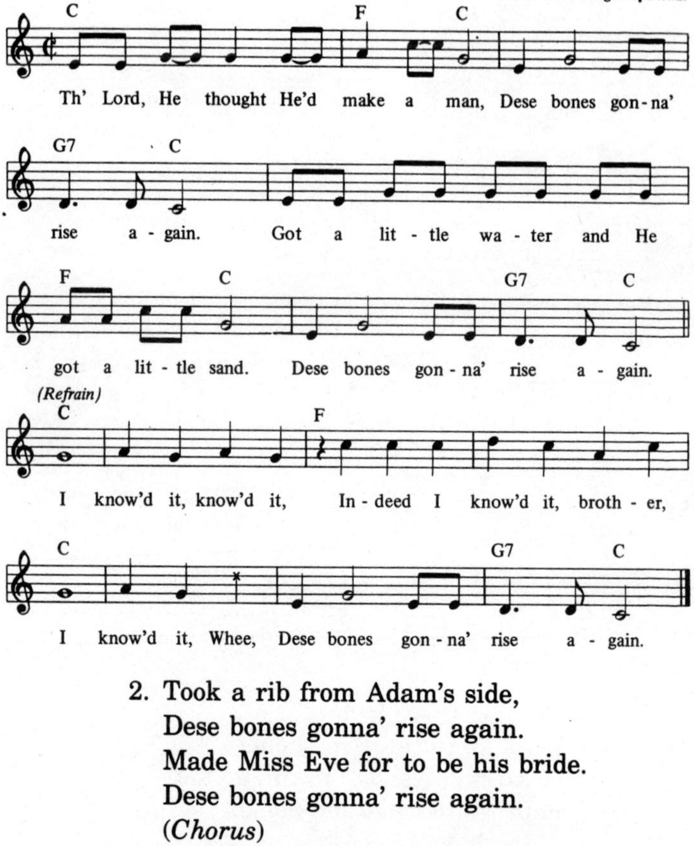
C F C
Th' Lord, He thought He'd make a man, Dese bones gon-na'
G7 C
rise a-gain. Got a lit-tle wa-ter and He
F C G7 C
got a lit-tle sand. Dese bones gon-na' rise a-gain.
(Refrain)
C F
I know'd it, know'd it, In-deed I know'd it, broth-er,
C G7 C
I know'd it, Whee, Dese bones gon-na' rise a-gain.

2. Took a rib from Adam's side,
   Dese bones gonna' rise again.
   Made Miss Eve for to be his bride.
   Dese bones gonna' rise again.
   (*Chorus*)

3. Put them in that garden fair, etc.,
   Thought they'd be contented there, etc.
   (*Chorus*)

4. Peaches, pears, and plums and such, etc.,
   That apple tree you must not touch, etc.
   (*Chorus*)

5. Ol' Miss Eve came a-walking 'round, etc.,
Spied that tree all loaded down, etc.
(*Chorus*)

6. Serpent coiled around the trunk, etc.,
At Miss Eve his eye he wunk, etc.
(*Chorus*)

7. First he give her one he pulled, etc.,
Then she filled her apron full, etc.
(*Chorus*)

8. Adam took a little slice, etc.,
Smacked his lips an' said, " 'Twas nice," etc.
(*Chorus*)

9. Th' Lord He come a-wand'rin roun', etc.,
Spied those peelin's on the groun'! etc.
(*Chorus*)

10. Adam, who them cores did leave, etc.,
Said, " 'Twarn't me, Lord, I speck 'twas Eve," etc.
(*Chorus*)

11. "Adam, y'all must leave this place, etc.,
What you done is a sad disgrace," etc.
(*Chorus*)

12. Gave him a hoe, and gave him a plow, etc.,
That's the reason we's workin' now, etc.
(*Chorus*)

Lord, I Want to Be a Christian

(Verse)

American Negro Spiritual

E B E
Lord, I want to be a Chris - tian In a my heart,
A E B C♯m
in a my heart, Lord, I want to be a Chris - tian
A E (Refrain) A
In a my heart. In a my heart,
In a my heart,
E A E
In a my heart, Lord, I
In a my heart,
B7 C♯m A E
want to be a Chris - tian In a my heart.

2. Lord, I want to be more loving
   In a my heart, in a my heart,
   Lord, I want to be more loving
   In a my heart.
   (*Refrain*)

3. Lord, I want to be more holy, etc.
4. I don't want to be like Judas, etc.
5. Lord, I want to be like Jesus, etc.

Go, Tell It on the Mountain

American Negro Spiritual

2. When I was a seeker,
I sought both night and day;
I asked my Lord to help me,
And he taught me to pray.
(*Refrain*)

3. He made me a watchman
Upon the city wall;
And if I am a Christian,
I am the least of all.
(*Refrain*)

4. It was in a lowly manger
That Jesus Christ was born;
The Lord sent down an angel
That bright and glorious morn.
(*Refrain*)

I've Got Shoes

American Negro Spiritual

Joyfully

Bb
I've got a robe, you've got a robe,
All of God's chil - dren got a robe:
Eb
When I get to heav - en, goin' to put on my robe,
Bb F7 Bb
Goin' to walk all o - ver God's heav - en.
(Refrain)
F Bb D Eb
Heav - en,* heav - en, ev - 'ry - bod - y talk - ing 'bout
Cm Eb Bb F
heav - en ain't go - ing there, heav - en, heav - en,
Bb F7 Bb D.C. Ending for last stanza
Goin' to shout all o - ver God's Heav - en, heav - en,
Repeat
F7 Bb
p
Goin' to shout all o - ver God's heav - en.

*End "heaven" with a humming sound.

2. I've got a crown, etc.,
   Goin' to shout all over God's heaven.
   (*Refrain*)

3. I've got a-shoes, etc.,
   Goin' to walk all over God's heaven.
   (*Refrain*)

4. I've got a harp, etc.,
   Goin' to play all over God's heaven.
   (*Refrain*)

5. I've got a song, etc.,
   Goin' to sing all over God's heaven.
   (*Refrain*)

Good-bye, Our God Is Watching O'er You

Wendell P. Loveless

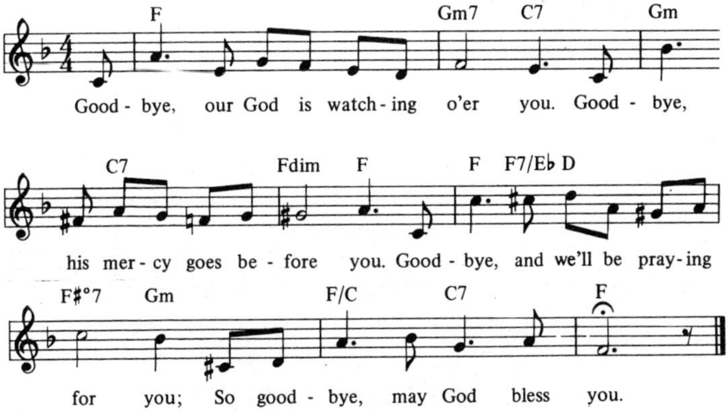
F Gm7 C7 Gm
Good - bye, our God is watch - ing o'er you. Good - bye,
C7 Fdim F F F7/Eb D
his mer - cy goes be - fore you. Good - bye, and we'll be pray - ing
F#°7 Gm F/C C7 F
for you; So good - bye, may God bless you.

That Old-time Religion

Traditional Spiritual

(Refrain)
G
Give me that old - time re - li - gion, Give me that
D7 G G7
old - time re - li - gion, Give me that old - time re -
C G D7 G Fine
li - gion, It's good e - nough for me.
(Verse)
G
It was good for old E - li - jah; It was
D7 G G7
good for old E - li - jah; It was good for old E -
C G D7 G D.C.
li - jah; And it's good e - nough for me.

2. It was good for the Hebrew children, etc.,
   And it's good enough for me.

3. It was good for old man Noah, etc.
4. It was good for the prophet Daniel, etc.
5. It was good for old Ezekiel, etc.
6. It was good for Paul and Silas, etc.
7. It was good for wise King Solomon, etc.

He's Got the Whole World in His Hands

Moderately and rhythmically

American Negro Spiritual

2. He's got the little bitty babies in his hands,
   He's got the little bitty babies in his hands,
   He's got the little bitty babies in his hands,
   He's got the whole world in his hands.

3. He's got you and me, brother, in his hands,
   He's got you and me, sister, in his hands,
   He's got you and me, brother, in his hands,
   He's got the whole world in his hands.

4. He's got the gamblin' man in his hands, etc.,
   He's got the whole world in his hands.

Whisper a Prayer

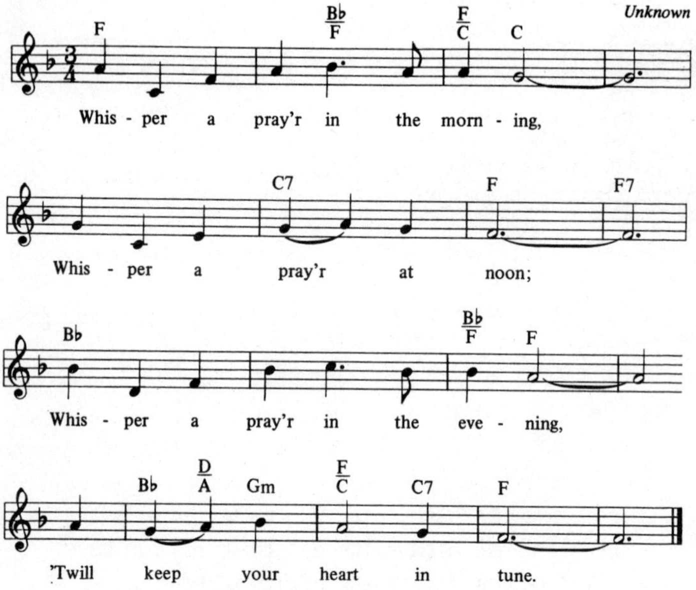
Unknown
F Bb/F F/C C
Whis - per a pray'r in the morn - ing,
C7 F F7
Whis - per a pray'r at noon;
Bb Bb/F F
Whis - per a pray'r in the eve - ning,
Bb D/A Gm F/C C7 F
'Twill keep your heart in tune.

2. God answers pray'r in the morning,
God answers pray'r at noon;
God answers pray'r in the evening,
He'll keep your heart in tune.

Lonesome Valley

American Folk Hymn

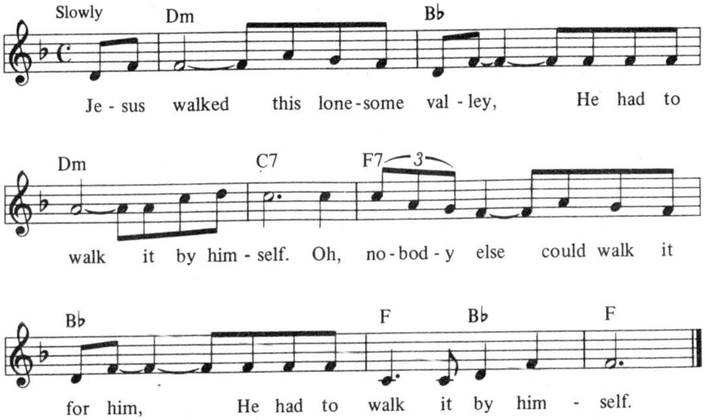
Slowly
Dm
Bb
Je - sus walked this lone-some val - ley, He had to
Dm
C7
F7 3
walk it by him - self. Oh, no-bod - y else could walk it
Bb
F
Bb
F
for him, He had to walk it by him - self.

2. You must go and stand your trial,
   You have to stand it by yourself.
   Oh, nobody else can stand it for you,
   You have to stand it by yourself.

3. We must walk this lonesome valley,
   We have to walk it by ourselves.
   Oh, nobody else can walk it for us,
   We have to walk it by ourselves.

Michael, Row the Boat Ashore

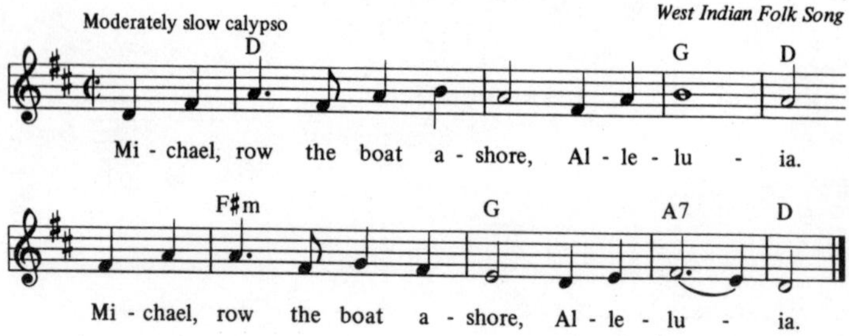
Moderately slow calypso
West Indian Folk Song
D G D
Mi - chael, row the boat a - shore, Al - le - lu - ia.
F♯m G A7 D
Mi - chael, row the boat a - shore, Al - le - lu - ia.

2. Michael's boat's a music boat, Alleluia,
   Michael's boat's a music boat, Alleluia.
3. Sister, help to trim the sail, Alleluia,
   Sister, help to trim the sail, Alleluia.
4. Jordan's River is chilly and cold, Alleluia,
   Kills the body but not the soul, Alleluia.
5. Jordan's River is deep and wide, Alleluia,
   Meet my mother on the other side, Alleluia.
6. Gabriel, blow the trumpet horn, Alleluia.
   Blow the trumpet loud and long, Alleluia.
7. Brother, lend a helping hand, Alleluia,
   Brother, lend a helping hand, Alleluia.
8. Michael's boat's a gospel boat, Alleluia,
   Michael's boat's a gospel boat, Alleluia.

Kum ba Yah
(Come by Here)

African Folk Song

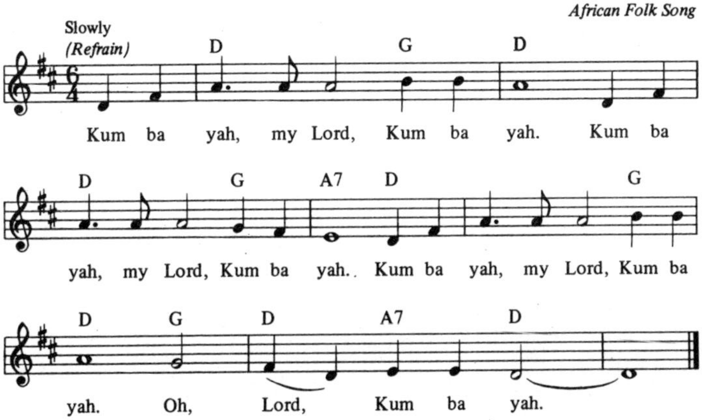
Slowly
(Refrain)
D G D
Kum ba yah, my Lord, Kum ba yah. Kum ba
D G A7 D G
yah, my Lord, Kum ba yah. Kum ba yah, my Lord, Kum ba
D G D A7 D
yah. Oh, Lord, Kum ba yah.

Verse (same tune as refrain):

1. Someone's crying, Lord, kum ba yah,
   Someone's crying, Lord, kum ba yah,
   Someone's crying, Lord, kum ba yah,
   Oh, Lord, kum ba yah.

2. Someone's singing, Lord, etc.
3. Someone's praying, etc.
4. Someone's hoping, etc.

Thou Wilt Keep Him in Perfect Peace

From Scripture

Anon. (Paul Beckwith, Arr.)

2. Marvel not that I say unto you, etc.,
   Ye must be born again.

3. Tho' your sins as scarlet be, etc.,
   They shall be white as snow.

4. If the Son shall make you free, etc.,
   Ye shall be free indeed.

5. They that wait upon the Lord, etc.,
   They shall renew their strength.

Steal Away

American Negro Spiritual

Moderately slow
(Refrain)
F C7 F
Steal a - way, steal a - way, Steal a - way to Je - sus.
C7 F Fine
Steal a - way, steal a - way home, I ain't got long to stay here.
(Verse)
Dm F
My Lord calls me; He calls me by the thun - der,
The trum - pet sounds with - in - a my soul;
C7 F D.C.
I ain't got long to stay here.

2. Green trees a-bending,
   Poor sinner stands a-trembling.
   The trumpet sounds with-in-a my soul,
   I ain't got long to stay here.

3. My Lord he calls me,
   He calls me by the lightning, etc.

4. Tombstones are bursting,
   Poor sinners stand a-trembling, etc.

Jacob's Ladder

American Spiritual

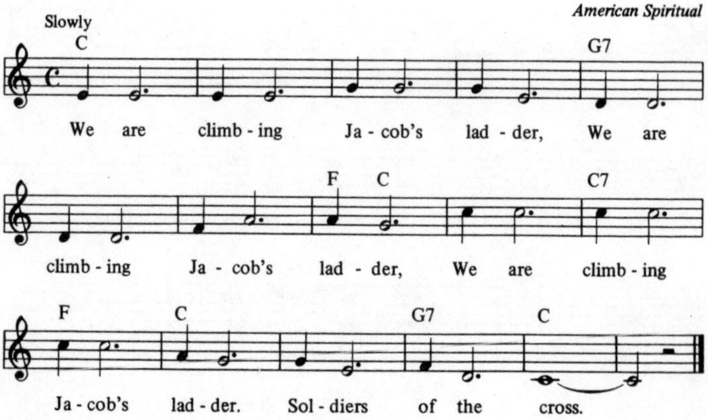

2. Every rung goes higher, higher, etc.,
   Soldiers of the cross.
3. Sinner, do you love my Jesus, etc.
4. If you love him, why not serve him, etc.
5. We are climbing higher, higher, etc.

BIBLIOGRAPHY

BOOKS

Costume

Barton, Lucy. *Appreciating Costume.* Boston: Walter H. Baker Co., 1969.

———. *Costuming the Biblical Play.* Boston: Walter H. Baker Co., 1937.

———. *Historic Costume for the Stage.* Boston: Walter H. Baker Co., 1961.

Fun Drama

Eisenberg, Helen, and Eisenberg, Larry. *The Handbook of Skits and Stunts.* New York: Association Press, 1953.

McGee, Cecil. *Drama for Fun.* Nashville: Broadman Press, 1969.

Makeup

Knapp, Jack Stuart. *The Technique of Stage Make-up.* Boston: Walter H. Baker Co., 1942.

Puppetry-Ventriloquism

Abbe, Dorothy. *The Dwiggins Marionettes: A Complete Experimental Theater in Miniature.* Boston: Plays, Inc., 1970.

Hill, Robert H. *You Can Be a Ventriloquist.* Chicago: Moody Press, 1974.

Reynolds, Joyce. *Puppet Shows That Reach and Teach Children.* Springfield, Mo.: Gospel Publishing House, 1972.

Robertson, Everett, ed. *Puppet Scripts for Use at Church.* Nashville: Sunday School Board of the Southern Baptist Convention, 1976.

———. *Using Puppetry in the Church.* Nashville: Sunday School Board of the Southern Baptist Convention, 1976.

Tichenor, Tom. *Tom Tichenor's Puppets.* Nashville: Abingdon Press, 1971.

Songbooks

America's Favorite Songs. New York: Putnam Publishing Group/Quick Fox, 1981.

Blankenship, Mark. *Singing Is Fun: Songs for Fellowship and Recreation.* Vol. 1. Nashville: Broadman Press, 1978.

———. *Singing Is Fun: Songs for Fellowship and Recreation.* Vol. 2. Nashville: Broadman Press, 1981.

Chase, Richard, ed. *Old Songs and Singing Games.* New York: Dover Books, 1973.

Collins, Fletcher. *Alamance Play-Party Songs and Singing Games.* Folklore Series. Norwood, Penna.: Norwood Editions, 1973.

Daring, Charles W., ed. *The New American Songster: Traditional Songs and Ballads of North America.* Washington, D.C.: University Press of America, 1983.

Ehret, Walter, and Evans, George K. *The International Book of Christmas Carols.* Brattleboro, Vt.: Greene Publishing Co., 1980.

Ehret, Walter, et al. *The International Book of Sacred Songs.* Englewood Cliffs, N.J.: Prentice-Hall, 1982.

Leisy, James. *The Good Times Songbook.* Nashville: Abingdon Press, 1974.

Rhys, Ernest, ed. *The New Golden Treasury of Songs and Lyrics.* Great Neck, N.Y.: Granger Books, 1977.

Religious Drama

Robertson, Everett. *Drama in Creative Worship.* Nashville: Convention Press, 1978.

———. *Extra Dimensions in Church Drama.* Nashville: Convention Press, 1977.

———. *Introduction to Church Drama.* Nashville: Convention Press, 1978.

———. *The Ministry of Clowning.* Nashville: Broadman Press, 1983.

Stage Direction

Dolman, John, and Knaub, Richard B. *The Art of Play Production.* New York: Harper & Row, 1973.

Welker, David. *Theatrical Direction: The Basic Techniques.* Boston: Allyn & Bacon, 1971.

Stage Scenery and Lighting

Bellman, Willard. *Lighting the Stage: Art and Practice.* San Francisco: Chandler, 1967.

Burris-Meyer, Harold, and Cole, Edward. *Scenery for the Theatre.* Boston: Little, Brown & Co., 1972.

Gillette, A. S. *Stage Scenery: Its Construction and Rigging.* Second edition. New York: Harper & Row, 1972.

SCRIPTS AND SUPPLIES

Abingdon Press
201 Eighth Avenue, South
Nashville, TN 37202

Anchorage Press
P.O. Box 8067
New Orleans, LA 70182

Baker's Plays
100 Chauncy Street
Boston, MA 02111

Broadman Press
127 Ninth Avenue, North
Nashville, TN 37234

The Coach House Press, Inc.
53 West Jackson Boulevard
Chicago, IL 60604

Contemporary Drama Service
Box 457
Downers Grove, IL 60515

Convention Press
127 Ninth Avenue, North
Nashville, TN 37234

Crescendo Publications, Inc.
P.O. Box 28218
2580 Gus Thomasson Road
Dallas, TX 75228

Drama Book Specialists
150 West 52nd Street
New York, NY 10019

Bibliography

The Dramatic Publishing Co.
86 E. Randolph Street
Chicago, IL 60601

Dramatists Play Service, Inc.
440 Park Avenue, South
New York, NY 10016

Heuer Publishing Co.
Box 248
Cedar Rapids, IA 52406

Lillenas Publishing Co.
P.O. Box 527
Kansas City, MO 64141

The Make-Up Center, Inc.
80 Boylston Street
Suite 420
Boston, MA 02116

Performance Publishing
978 North McLean
Boulevard
Elgin, IL 60120

Pioneer Drama Service
2172 S. Colorado Boulevard
Denver, CO 80222

Samuel French, Inc.
25 West 45th Street
New York, NY 10036

Stage Magic Plays
Box 246
Schulenburg, TX 78956

The Sunday School Board of
the Southern Baptist
Convention
127 Ninth Avenue, North
Nashville, TN 37234

Theatrical Makeup
902 Broadway
New York, NY 10010

Word, Inc.
Box 1790
Waco, TX 76703

INDEX BY CATEGORY

INDEX OF SONG TITLES